THE CIVIL WAR

"A House Divided"

Zachary Kent

—American War Series—

Enslow Publishers, Inc.

40 Industrial Road	PO Box 38
Box 398	Aldershot
Berkeley Heights, NJ 07922	Hants GU12 6BP
USA	UK

http://www.enslow.com

"A house divided against itself cannot stand. I believe this government cannot endure permanently, half slave and half free. I do not expect the Union to be dissolved—I do not expect the house to fall; but I do expect it will cease to be divided."
—Abraham Lincoln, June 16, 1858.
Acceptance speech after nomination as candidate for the U.S. Senate.

Copyright © 1994 by Zachary Kent

Library of Congress Cataloging-in-Publication Data

Kent, Zachary.
   The Civil War: "a house divided" / Zachary Kent.
      p. cm. — (American war series)
   Includes bibliographical references and index.
   ISBN 0-7660-1728-1 (pbk)
   ISBN 0-89490-522-8 (library ed.)
      1. United States—History—Civil War, 1861-1865—Juvenile
literature. [1. United States—History—Civil War, 1861-1865.]
   I. Title. II. Series.
   E468.K36 1994
   973.7—dc20   93-33622
                                                CIP
                                                 AC
Printed in the United States of America

10 9 8

To Our Readers: We have done our best to make sure all Internet addresses in this book were active and appropriate when we went to press. However, the author and the publisher have no control over and assume no liability for the material available on those Internet sites or on other Web sites they may link to. Any comments or suggestions can be sent by e-mail to comments@enslow.com or to the address on the back cover.

Illustration Credits:
Courtesy of the Prints and Photographs Division, Library of Congress: pp. 7, 10, 14, 26, 29, 40, 44, 46, 50, 52, 53, 58, 60, 61, 62, 71, 78, 80, 81, 85, 91, 92, 97, 99, 100, 106, 115; Enslow Publishers, Inc., pp. 20, 34, 48; National Archives: pp. 17, 22, 24, 31, 33, 43, 64, 68, 75, 88, 104, 108, 113, 118.

Cover Illustration:
Courtesy of the Prints and Photographs Division, Library of Congress.

Contents

Foreword

The photograph of an old man hangs on a living-room wall in my father's house. The man is George W. March, my great-great-grandfather. His hair is white and neatly combed. He has a long white beard, and his blue eyes shine with pride. Pinned on the front of his coat is the star-shaped medal awarded to Union veterans of the American Civil War.

As a boy, I listened to the stories my grandmother told me about "Grandpa" March. He fought with a Pennsylvania cavalry regiment and had horses shot from under him in battle. As a grown-up I have visited many of the great battlefields. At Farmville, Virginia, I walked along the road where Grandpa March was captured during a cavalry charge on April 7, 1865. The Civil War is very real to me because it is part of my family heritage.

I believe no war ever touched as many American lives as did the Civil War. Between 1861 and 1865 the Northern states and the Southern states clashed in a struggle to decide the future of the nation. America's husbands, sons, and fathers marched off to war. Some 3,000,000 men would serve in the Union and Confederate armies. And after the last shot was fired, over 600,000 soldiers lay in graves. The Civil War claimed more American lives—from battle and disease—than World War I, World War II, Vietnam, and all of our other wars combined. Entire cities were burned to the ground. The boom of cannon and the crack of rifle fire turned peaceful woods and farmlands into landscapes of blood and horror. Even today the evidence of the Civil War remains on scarred battlefields, in vivid photographs, and in the thrilling memories passed down from generation to generation.

"I did not know that one could live such days of excitement. . . . Everybody tells you half of something, and then rushes off to tell something else, or to hear the last news."
—Charleston citizen Mary Boykin Chestnut, April 13, 1861

1 Storm Over Fort Sumter

 "Fort Sumter!" Newspaper headlines blared the name, and most Americans spoke of Fort Sumter in the spring of 1861. Along the waterfront of Charleston, South Carolina, angry citizens shook their fists out toward the sea. On an island at the mouth of the harbor three miles away, Fort Sumter stood proud and alone. Above its high brick walls the red, white, and blue of the United States flag snapped boldly in the breeze.

America tottered on the brink of civil war. Already South Carolina, Mississippi, Alabama, Georgia, Florida, Louisiana, and Texas had quit the Union. Together they formed the new Confederate States of America. Across the South, Confederate soldiers were seizing federal arsenals, forts, and navy dockyards.

In Charleston, tensions mounted day after day. For weeks Southern militiamen arrived by train. Excitedly, these soldiers marched through the streets and pitched their tents outside the city. The Confederates demanded Fort Sumter. The United States government refused to give it up. "Strike a blow!" Southern politician Roger Pryor urged one cheering Charleston crowd. Gray-haired Major Robert Anderson commanded the small Union garrison at Fort Sumter. Nine officers, 68 enlisted soldiers, 8 army musicians, and 43 civilian workmen (carpenters and bricklayers making repairs at the fort), a total of 128 men, obeyed Anderson's orders.

Along the shoreline surrounding Fort Sumter, 6,000 Confederate soldiers occupied Fort Moultrie, Fort Johnson, and other military positions. Brigadier General P. G. T. Beauregard of Louisiana commanded this Southern force. Beauregard knew Major Anderson well. More than twenty years earlier as a West Point army cadet, Beauregard had learned his gunnery skills in an artillery class taught by Anderson. Now dozens of Confederate cannon pointed toward Fort Sumter. Gazing through binoculars, Major Anderson understood the growing danger. "The clouds are threatening," he grimly wrote, "and the storm may break at any moment."

In the early morning blackness of April 12, 1861, three Confederate officers on General Beauregard's staff rowed a boat across the murky waters of the harbor. Stepping ashore at Fort Sumter, they demanded the surrender of the Union garrison. Major Anderson refused. One of the Confederate officers scribbled a note and

The attack on Fort Sumter, April 12-13, 1861. A Confederate battery fires away. Some Confederate gun crews first heated their cannonballs in ovens. "Hot shots" fired into Fort Sumter caused wooden barracks to go up in flames.

presented it to Anderson. "By authority of Brigadier General Beauregard . . . " it read, "we have the honor to notify you that he will open . . . fire . . . on Fort Sumter in one hour from this time.[1] The Southern officers rowed back to shore, and Major Anderson tensely waited. The moment of terrible confrontation had arrived.

At 4:30 A.M., Confederate Lieutenant Henry S. Farley jerked the lanyard of a cannon at Fort Johnson on James Island. A signal shell was sent soaring through the sky with a roar. One hundred feet above Fort Sumter the shell burst in an explosion of flame. Many people had expected a fight. Still the sudden noise startled Charleston citizen Mary Chesnut. "I sprang out of bed," she later exclaimed, "and on my knees . . . I prayed as I have never prayed before." Confederate Captain Stephen Lee recalled that the first shot "brought every soldier in the harbor to his feet, and every man, woman, and child in the City of Charleston from their beds."[2]

Over the next hours, the bombardment became deafening as every Confederate cannon joined in. The constant firing lit up the harbor sky. Union Sergeant James Chester observed, "shot and shell went screaming over Sumter as if an army of devils were swooping around it." Not until 7:00 A.M. did the Union soldiers respond to the attack. Then the officer on duty, Captain Abner Doubleday, ordered Sumter's guns to return fire. It was too dangerous to work the heavy Union cannon exposed on the open upper level of the fort. Within the fort's sheltered lower level, however, twenty-one cannon stood ready for action. "Our firing now became regular,"

Captain Doubleday later recalled, "and was answered from the rebel guns which encircled us."

Cannonballs and artillery shells poured into the fort. Smashed bricks went flying and mortar dust clouded the air. Great shells buried themselves into the parade ground, making the earth shake. The fort suffered, declared Sergeant Chester, "a perfect hurricane of shot." In Charleston, citizens watched the thrilling spectacle from their rooftops. They jammed the wharves for a view and crowded onto the beaches. "Boom, boom, goes the cannon all the time," exclaimed Mary Chesnut. "The nervous strain is awful."[3]

Through the day and into the night, the Confederates continued firing. Still Fort Sumter held out. Reported Confederate General Beauregard, "Our brave troops . . . cheered the garrison for its pluck and gallantry." On the morning of the second day, April 13, Union Captain Doubleday remembered, "One fifth of the fort was on fire." The fire crept toward the fort's powder magazine. Soldiers quickly rushed inside. They gasped for breath as they rolled barrels of gunpowder to safety through smoke and flame. While the men were busy with this dangerous work, nearly all of the cannon inside the fort fell silent.

In the early afternoon enemy gunfire snapped the Fort Sumter flagstaff, but exclaimed Sergeant Chester, "the old flag was rescued and nailed to a new staff . . . [and] was carried to the ramparts." Finally at about 1:30 P.M. Major Anderson hauled down the flag. He ordered a white bedsheet raised in its place. His weary soldiers could endure no more. After 33 hours and the crash of

Inside battered Fort Sumter brick and stone rubble lay in piles. For the next four years the Confederacy would control the fort.

3,341 shells on the island fortress, the Union commander called for a truce. Confederate officers were stunned when they saw the battered fort close up. The crumbling walls were pitted by cannonballs. The main gate was smashed to splinters. Brick staircases lay in ruined heaps. Rubble was everywhere, and dust and smoke choked the air. Confederate Captain Stephen Lee also remembered, "Major Anderson, his officers, and his men were blackened by smoke and cinders, and showed signs of fatigue and exhaustion."[4] By a miracle no one had been killed or seriously wounded on either side during the fight.

By 7:00 P.M. terms of surrender were agreed upon. That night in Charleston, church bells rang, ladies waved handkerchiefs, and men happily danced in the streets. Southerners regarded the capture of Fort Sumter as a great victory in their fight for independence. The date of April 14, 1861 marked the official day of surrender. Drummers beat the notes of "Yankee Doodle" as the Union troops marched across the parade ground past the piles of rubble and through the dust and smoke. Last to leave the fort was a solemn Major Robert Anderson. Tucked beneath his arm was the fort's tattered United States flag. Four years of bloody fighting lay ahead before the Stars and Stripes would again fly above Fort Sumter's ramparts.

"Civil war is actually upon us," Ohio senator John Sherman declared in shock when he heard of the fort's surrender.

American poet Walt Whitman sadly wrote, "All the past we leave behind."

Hurrah! Hurrah!
For Southern Rights Hurrah!
      —from the Southern song "The Bonnie Blue Flag"

2 Brother Against Brother

 The American colonists who fought for independence during the Revolutionary War shared a common history. Together they formed a new nation, full of hope and promise. By the mid-1800s, however, the northern and southern parts of that nation began drifting in different directions. The great moral issue of slavery threatened to tear the United States apart.

King Cotton

"Cotton is King," declared South Carolina senator James Hammond in the 1850s, "and the African must be a slave, or there's an end of all things, and soon." America's first shackled African slaves arrived at Jamestown, Virginia, in 1619. Across the South sweating slaves picked tobacco, cut rice, and chopped sugar cane.

Although cotton grew well in the warmest southern states, the difficulty of handpicking the clinging seeds from the cotton fiber made that crop unprofitable.

Then in 1793 Eli Whitney, a clever Connecticut schoolteacher, visited Mulberry Grove, a plantation near Savannah, Georgia. Within a few weeks Whitney had invented a simple engine whose rollers, teeth, and brushes made cotton-cleaning easy. Whitney's cotton "gin" caused a remarkable transformation throughout the South. In 1790, the United States produced fewer than 9,000 bales of cotton. By 1860 almost five million bales were harvested in the South, fully seven-eighths of the world's cotton.

Only about one-quarter of the whites in the South actually owned slaves. Most Southern farmers raised cattle, corn, and other crops by their own hard labor. The increased use of slaves, however, made some Southerners very wealthy. Inside great plantation houses, slaves served as butlers, cooks, and maids. Their labors allowed the master and his family to live in gracious comfort. Outside, on many plantations, overseers armed with whips kept slave field hands working. By 1860 more than three million slaves toiled in the South.

Life was very different in the Northern states. Irish, German, and other European immigrants flooded into the country. They gladly took manufacturing jobs, working at low wages. Machinery thumped and whined in busy Northern shoe factories and textile mills. The telegraph, the sewing machine, the mechanical reaper, and other Northern inventions created thriving new

COME ONE!
COME ALL!

Richmond, Burke, Jefferson, Columbia, Warren, Wilkes, Edgefield and Barnwell,

Come to the Sale of my LIKELY NEGROES,

☞ SEE SHERIFF'S ADVERTISEMENT. ☜

Made by the late Major George L. Twiggs, whom the Attorney, Col. Cumming, and the sons, have lifted from the grave to levy on and sell the little remnant of negroes left me, under the cruelty of my father-in-law, who stood at the market-house and bid on the only negro I requested to be bought in for me, and made him cost me $200 more than he would have brought; and that too, after for many summers having risked my life, going from home at four o'clock in the morning, returning at 9 o'clock at night, breathing the malaria of wet swamps, from decaying vegetable matter, attending to his planting interest, when he was away spending his summers in pleasurable delights, having for years fed, clothed and schooled his off-cast son, daughter-in-law, and all their children. Read the pamphlet and behold the base and horrible ingratitude of this cast-off son, G. W. L. Twiggs, now one of his Executors, and behold how he repays me for my acts of kindness in saving for him, as the records of the Court will show, about $20,000, when he had not a friend left him on earth. See him and his brother John, the other Executor, and left the guardian and trustee (in whom their father never had any confidence, till penance was due,) of my wife and children, to take care of them, virtually, under the arm of the law, come forward to rob my children in these trying times, when the best 30 day drafts bring 1¼ per cent. Come see them, after having under the judgment cost me $10,000 in actual cash and sacrifices of property, besides preventing me from making $40,000 more, proceed to sell five negroes, worth, with such resources as I have, (being most of them mechanics,) to me $500 each year, equal to 2,500 per annum, to loan, I suppose, to Mr. Rambo, the father-in-law, $3,500 at 7 per cent, $245 interest, (who did have $7,000 at 7 per cent. of my wife's money,) making a difference to my children of $2,255 per annum above the interest. There is no error in this calculation; it is too true. And thus would they destroy my poor children, because the father will not bow down and lick the dust off their feet, under an unholy will. After the miserable abuse of me and my property, under the judgment, the cry is, my second son must be taken from school and put to work, because the estate, under the most unskilful and bad management of the brother, John D. Twiggs, (my master, under the unholy will,) is not able to educate my children. I will take any estate equal to it, and after one year make it produce $10,000 per annum. This is only what was before done under the *cruelty of the father, and base ingratitude and horrible treachery* of their uncle, D. E. Twiggs, U. S. A.

Come! come! all come to the sale, and you will have a bid at a most excellent nurse, the nurse of my baby, who loved her as much as he did his mother, exposed to the Sheriff's hammer by Mrs. C.'s own brothers. Come, you grandfathers who love your grandchildren more than the poor Major ever did his, bid strong for this woman, and present her to the youngest one. There will be, likewise, other negroes for sale, as Doyle the Sheriff, informs you. I have let the Attorney and sons play along under their malicious persecutions, till I could hang them up before the world as you now see them. The agony will soon be over. The Twiggs' will have more of Benton's yellow boys, and their hearts will sink within them when they behold me, while I will have that enjoyment, peace of mind and happiness, not one ounce of which have I enjoyed for the last five years.

The agony will soon be over, unless they draw again their double barrel guns and shoot me for daring to speak the truth. Come see! For the sake of gold, they would crush a brother-in-law; nay, more, they would even drive daggers to the hearts of the children of him who never faltered, in the hour of their deep distress, to such ungrateful men as George W. L. Twiggs, (read pamphlet) and the distinguished Major General D. E. Twiggs, U. S. A.

Come see them, in "my deep distress,"—the Attorney and sons—hang up themselves and the departed dead in infamy before the world, by the fiendish persecutions of me, the son-in-law, and brother-in-law of this Twiggs family.

Come one, come all, and, as poor old Major Twiggs remarked after the sale and sacrifice of my most valuable property under the sheriff's hammer, in 1852,— "By George! he stood it like a man—as fast as one negro was sold he had another ready!"—and you will see I will have another ready to answer to the fiendish persecutions of his malicious sons.

JAMES L. COLEMAN.

Augusta, Ga., Dec. 26, 1856.

An invitation to a slave auction.

industries. By 1860 the North possessed ten times as many factories as the South. Northerners had no use for slavery.

Abolition!

"I *will* be harsh as truth,"exclaimed Boston publisher William Lloyd Garrison. "I will not retreat a single inch—and *I will be heard.*" In 1831 Garrison began printing an antislavery newspaper called *The Liberator.* The cruelty of Southern slavery deeply angered Garrison and other Northerners. They demanded that slavery be abolished. A runaway Maryland slave named Frederick Douglass gained fame as a public speaker for abolition. Douglass liked to tell audiences, "I appear this evening as a thief and robber. I stole this head, these limbs, this body from my master and ran off with them."[1] Like Garrison, Douglass published an antislavery newspaper. He called it *North Star* because at night runaway slaves often used the North Star as their guide to freedom.

A secret organization called the "Underground Railroad" helped many runaways escape to Canada. Hiding in safe houses along the way, some 100,000 slaves fled northward. One of the bravest and best known "conductors" on the Underground Railroad was Harriet Tubman. A Maryland slave who ran away in 1849, Tubman earned the nickname "Moses" by leading more than 300 slaves to freedom over the years.

News of slave whippings, and sad stories of slave families being broken up and members sold at auctions upset many Northerners. In 1852 Harriet Beecher Stowe wrote *Uncle Tom's Cabin* after a visit to the slave state of Kentucky. The best-selling novel, which described the suffering of slaves, sold 300,000 copies in the United States within a year.

By 1854 thousands of Northern abolitionists vowed to stop the spread of slavery. That year Congress's Kansas-Nebraska Act promised settlers they could decide if slavery should be allowed in Kansas. Northern abolitionists rushed into that western territory and fought Southern slaveowning settlers. Over two hundred people died in skirmishes to determine the future of "Bleeding Kansas."

The fight for abolition filled one Kansas settler with special rage. In a mad attempt to free all slaves, fifty-nine-year-old John Brown led five black and thirteen white men on a raid into Harper's Ferry, Virginia, on Sunday evening, October 16, 1859. Brown and his raiders seized the federal armory, arsenal, and engine house, and rounded up hostages. By a strange twist of fate, as fighting broke out the first man shot by Brown's men was the town baggage master, Shephard Hayward, a freed slave. On Tuesday morning 90 U.S. marines, commanded by Colonel Robert E. Lee, arrived from Washington, D.C. The marines charged the engine house, battered down the door, and captured the surviving raiders. The entire fight had cost seventeen lives, including those of two of Brown's sons.

Many Northerners expressed sympathy for John Brown. Southerners, however, were outraged by his raid. Found guilty of murder, treason, and rebellion, Brown

John Brown. From a mural by artist John Stewart Curry. While in Kansas, John Brown vowed, "There will be no more peace in this land until slavery is done for." His raid into Harper's Ferry, Virginia in October 1859 shocked the nation.

gave a prediction about America's future. Before his hanging in Charles Town, Virginia, on December 2, 1859, he handed a note to his guard: "I, John Brown, am now quite *certain* that the crimes of this *guilty* land will never be purged away but with Blood."[2]

"A House Divided"

"There is a settled gloom hanging over everyone here," wrote Varina Davis, wife of Mississippi senator Jefferson Davis in Washington, D.C. By the late 1850s the slavery question had driven an ugly wedge between the North and South. At the Capitol, congressmen carried guns and knives in case of fierce arguments. Southerners openly talked of taking their states out of the Union to protect their right to continue slavery.

In 1858 the nation's attention turned toward the senatorial campaign being waged in Illinois. The contest pitted Republican Abraham Lincoln against Democrat Stephen A. Douglas. Lincoln was a humble man who had been a river boatman, storekeeper, and surveyor and later became a successful Springfield, Illinois, lawyer. His old friend Stephen Douglas was the best-known senator in the United States. Seven times in seven Illinois counties the two candidates met to debate. In simple and forceful language Lincoln argued against slavery. Earlier he had warned:

> A house divided against itself cannot stand. I believe this government cannot endure permanently half slave and half free.

In the end Lincoln lost the senate election by a close

margin. But the Lincoln-Douglas Debates had made him famous throughout the country. Impressed Republican politicians nominated Lincoln for president in 1860. In a heated four-way race, Lincoln ran against Stephen A. Douglas, John C. Breckinridge of Kentucky, and John Bell of Tennessee. When the November election votes were finally tallied, Americans learned that "Honest Abe" Lincoln had won.

As the news spread, Northerners rejoiced. The poet Henry W. Longfellow wrote in his diary, "Lincoln is elected. . . . This is a great victory. . . . Freedom is triumphant." Angry Southerners, however, feared that Lincoln surely would abolish slavery. The Augusta, Georgia, *Constitution* exclaimed, "The South should arm at once." The United States was on the brink of its greatest crisis. Many Southerners felt Lincoln's victory gave them no choice but to leave the Union.

On December 20, 1860, the state government of South Carolina voted to secede from the Union. Within the next month Mississippi, Florida, Alabama, Georgia, Louisiana, and Texas also seceded. Delegates from the seceded states gathered at the Exchange Hotel in Montgomery, Alabama. These Southern leaders quickly drafted a Southern constitution. On February 9, 1861, they unanimously elected Jefferson Davis president of the new Confederate States of America.

"Forward to Richmond!"

"In your hands, my dissatisfied countrymen, and not in mine is the momentous issue of civil war," declared

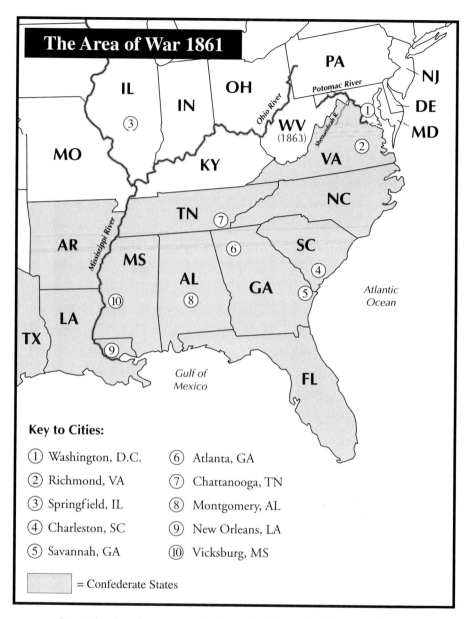

The Area of War 1861

Key to Cities:

① Washington, D.C. ⑥ Atlanta, GA

② Richmond, VA ⑦ Chattanooga, TN

③ Springfield, IL ⑧ Montgomery, AL

④ Charleston, SC ⑨ New Orleans, LA

⑤ Savannah, GA ⑩ Vicksburg, MS

☐ = Confederate States

By 1861, Southern states had seceded from the Union to form the Confederacy. The shaded area shows the division of the United States.

Abraham Lincoln at his inauguration as the sixteenth U.S. president on March 4, 1861. "We are not enemies but friends. We must not be enemies."[3]

The South refused to listen. In April, Confederate soldiers attacked Fort Sumter. Abraham Lincoln understood his duty. He must hold the United States together. Instantly, he called for 75,000 volunteers to put down the Southern rebellion. Rather than fight their sister slaveholding states, Virginia, North Carolina, Arkansas, and Tennessee swiftly quit the Union and joined the Confederacy.

Now that war had begun, the people of Washington, D.C., felt nervous. Only the Potomac River separated that city from the enemy in Virginia. Northern state militias hastened southward to save the capital. In Massachusetts, Mary Ashton Livermore observed, "Everywhere the drum and fife thrilled the air with their stirring call. Recruiting offices were opened in every city, town, and village . . . and the streets [echoed with] the measured tread of soldiers."[4]

Thousands of Southerners also rushed off to fight. Explained George A. Gibbs, a Mississippi boy, "Nothing would do me but to enlist. My parents pleaded with me, saying I was too young to go to war. . . . But nothing could shake my resolution to be a soldier."

As the first Northern volunteers reached Washington, housing was scarce. Some Rhode Island men camped in the Patent Office. Hundreds of New York troops found shelter in the Senate Chamber, while a Massachusetts regiment lodged in the Capitol Rotunda.

Still dressed in civilian clothes, soldiers of the Cassius M. Clay Battalion defend the White House in April 1861. During the first weeks of the war northern volunteers rushed to Washington, D.C., to protect the federal government.

Union camps encircled the city. "You can go up into the dome of the Capitol and see tents of the Federal army in every direction as far as you can see," Militiaman Augustus Woodbury wrote home.

On May 24, 1861, Colonel Elmer Ellsworth led his New York regiment across the Potomac River to Alexandria, Virginia. At the Marshall House hotel Ellsworth pulled down a Rebel flag. Angered, the Confederate hotel owner, James Jackson, killed Ellsworth with a shotgun blast. As his tearful troops carried his body home, Ellsworth became the first tragic war hero of the North.

In June, the Confederate government moved to Richmond, Virginia. In the pages of the *New York Tribune,* editor Horace Greeley exclaimed, "Forward to Richmond! Forward to Richmond! The Rebel Congress must not be allowed to meet there on the twentieth of July!" In response to Northern demands for action, Lincoln ordered an advance south. Under command of Brigadier General Irvin McDowell, an army of 35,000 inexperienced Union troops marched into Virginia on July 16, 1861. The soldiers tramped along in high spirits at the start of their great adventure. "They stopped every moment to pick blackberries or get water," McDowell unhappily declared; "they would not keep in the ranks."

First Battle of Bull Run

Twenty miles southwest of Washington stood an important Virginia railroad junction at the town of Manassas, Virginia. After his victory at Fort Sumter, General P. G. T. Beauregard received command of the Confederate

Jefferson Davis (1808-1889) President of the Confederate States of America. "I . . . will not shrink from the task imposed on me," he stated after taking office. As the head of the South's new government he named cabinet officers, appointed military officers, and planned government policies.

army of 20,000 men gathered near Manassas. Along a crooked stream called Bull Run the Confederates awaited the Union attack.

On July 18, McDowell tested the Confederate lines at a crossing called Blackburn's Ford. "Suddenly there comes a volley from beneath the green foliage along the winding stream, and the air is thick with leaden rain," reported Boston newsman Charles Coffin.[5] Pushing his brigade forward, Union Colonel William T. Sherman was shocked. "For the first time in my life I saw cannonballs strike men and crash through the trees and saplings above and around us."

After scouting the area for two more days, McDowell attacked across Sudley Springs Ford on the morning of July 21. The night before, Beauregard had received trainloads of reinforcements. These men were part of General Joseph E. Johnston's 11,000 Confederates being hastily transferred from Virginia's Shenandoah Valley. For the first time in history, railroads played a vital military role.

Around 9:30 A.M. the Yankee troops charged toward the Warrenton Turnpike. Brave Confederate soldiers countercharged. Across the open fields, men lunged forward through the gunsmoke. By late morning, unable to hold off the strong Union advance, Georgia and South Carolina troops retreated up Henry House Hill. At the brow of the hill, Brigadier General Bernard Bee saw a fresh Virginia brigade commanded by Brigadier General Thomas J. Jackson standing in a solid line. "Look," Bee shouted to his weary Confederates. "There is Jackson standing like a stone wall! Rally behind the Virginians!"

Through the next bloody hours Jackson's line held, and he gained a legendary nickname: "Stonewall" Jackson.

The battle seesawed back and forth beneath the blazing summer sun. In a murky fog of gunsmoke, amid whizzing bullets and shrieking horses, the Union troops became confused. Behind the Confederate lines, General Johnson met Brigadier General Edmund Kirby-Smith's brigade, which had just arrived on the Manassas trains.

The 69th New York Regiment rushes toward Confederate cannon on Henry House Hill. "...it was impossible to stand long in that fire," Union Colonel William T. Sherman declared afterwards. The fact that some Union militiamen at Bull Run wore gray uniforms and some Confederates wore blue added to the battle confusion. Later in the war, Northern troops would dress in a standard blue uniform. The Southerners would wear gray or "butternut" brown.

"Take them to the front," yelled Johnston. "Go where the fire is hottest." The added strength of these and other Confederate reinforcements proved too much for the Yankees. The exhausted Northern soldiers suddenly broke and ran for the rear.

From Henry House Hill, Confederate Lieutenant William Blackford observed that suddenly "the whole field was a confused swarm of men, like bees, running away as fast as their legs could carry them."[6] Swept up in the sudden Union retreat were many ladies and gentlemen from Washington, D.C., who had ridden down to watch the battle from the safety of the hills north of Bull Run. Along the Warrenton Turnpike toward Washington, soldiers and civilians rushed in fear. Horses and carriages clogged the road. Frightened Union soldiers threw away their guns and knapsacks in order to run faster. Behind them on the Bull Run battlefield lay the bodies of 481 Union and 387 Confederate soldiers. The fight had been bloody, but Southerners were thrilled with their victory. "We have taught them a lesson in their invasion of the sacred soil of Virginia," declared Jefferson Davis.

In Washington clouds of gloom darkened the streets. McDowell's beaten men trudged back through a drizzle of rain. At the White House President Lincoln spent a sleepless night, but by morning he was even more determined to continue the fight. Instead of making a quick end to the war, the Battle of Bull Run only marked the beginning.

*Whatever nation gets . . . control of the Ohio,
Mississippi, and Missouri Rivers, will control
the continent.*
　—Union Brigadier General William Tecumseh Sherman

3　War in the West

As war fever gripped the nation, command-ing U.S. Army General Winfield Scott sug-gested crushing the Southern rebellion the same way the great Anaconda snake encircles and squeezes the life out of its victims. Scott's "Anaconda Plan" called for Union forces to capture the Mississippi River, while Union war-ships formed a coastal blockade of Southern ports.

Unconditional Surrender

"The South will fight," thirty-eight-year-old Ulysses S. Grant correctly guessed. In April 1861, Grant worked as a humble clerk in his father's leather-goods store in Ga-lena, Illinois. Grant's military education at West Point and his Mexican War experience, however, earned him a brigadier general's commission in August of 1861. Soon he commanded all of the Union troops gathering in southern Illinois.

With War Department approval, Grant prepared to attack two Confederate strongholds—Forts Henry and Donelson—in Tennessee. With 17,000 men and U.S. Navy gunboats as escort, Grant steamed up the Tennessee River. A powerful naval bombardment forced the Confederates to abandon Fort Henry on February 6, 1862. The Rebels retreated overland twelve miles to Fort Donelson on the Cumberland River. Promptly, Grant marched his army over the frozen roads and surrounded Fort Donelson.

On February 15, Rebel troops charged out of the fort and struck at the right side of the Union lines. Arriving

According to General Winfield Scott's "Anaconda Plan," a U.S. naval blockade along the Atlantic and Gulf coasts would help strangle the Confederate economy. At the same time, Union troops would capture the Mississippi River.

at that part of the field, Grant quickly grasped the situation. To his shaken men he shouted, "Fill your cartridge boxes quick, and get into line; the enemy is trying to escape and he must not be permitted to do so." Cheered by this news, the Yankees rallied and with tough fighting closed up their lines again. Brigadier General Charles F. Smith launched the Union counterattack. "Come on, you volunteers, come on," he shouted. "This is your chance. You volunteered to be killed for love of your country and now you can be."

With no hope of escape, on February 16 Confederate Brigadier General Simon Bolivar Buckner sent a message through the lines, asking for favorable surrender terms. Grant quickly responded with a note of his own. "No terms," it bluntly stated, "except an unconditional and immediate surrender can be accepted. I propose to move immediately upon your works."[1] Caving in to Grant's demand, Buckner surrendered his entire army of some 15,000 men.

The Union reclaimed control of the Tennessee and Cumberland rivers and the heart of western Tennessee. "The news of the fall of Fort Donelson," Grant later remembered, "caused great delight all over the North." It was easily the greatest Union victory of the war so far. Everywhere people spoke proudly of General U. S. Grant. "Unconditional Surrender" Grant they called him now.

Shiloh

During the next weeks, Grant's army pushed south to

Ulysses S. Grant (1822-1885) At Fort Donelson, Tennessee he earned the nickname "Unconditional Surrender." President Lincoln quickly rewarded the hard fighting Union officer with a promotion to major general.

clear the last of the Confederates out of western Tennessee. On Sunday morning April 6, 1862, 42,000 Union troops were encamped in wooded ravines on the west side of the Tennessee River near Pittsburg Landing, Tennessee. In a desperate attempt to halt the Union advance, Confederate General Albert Sidney Johnston mounted a surprise attack with a Rebel army of 30,000 men.

With piercing shouts, known as "Rebel Yells," the Confederates charged into the Union camps from the south at about 9:30 A.M.. Cannon shells screamed through the air near a crude log church called the Shiloh Meeting House. Thousands of stunned Union soldiers retreated in wide-eyed panic all the way to the muddy Tennessee riverbank. "We were crowding them," Rebel soldier Sam Watkins later recalled. "We were jubilant; we were triumphant. . . . The Federal dead and wounded covered the ground."[2]

Along the battlefront, in thick woods and dense underbrush, the fighting roared on in savage confusion. Ten-year-old Union drummer boy John Clem of the 12th Michigan Regiment became famous as "Johnny Shiloh" after an artillery shell smashed his instrument. Crouched along a sunken road, the men of Union Brigadier General Benjamin Prentiss' division stoutly resisted all enemy attacks. Bullets flew so thickly along the road that it became known as the "Hornets' Nest."

More hard fighting took place in a nearby peach orchard where General Johnston himself led one Rebel charge. Soon afterward, a bullet thudded into Johnston's right leg behind his knee. The bullet cut an artery, and

Union drummer boy John Clem survived the Battle of Shiloh and many other engagements fought in the west. After the war, he remained in the U.S. Army and rose to the rank of major general.

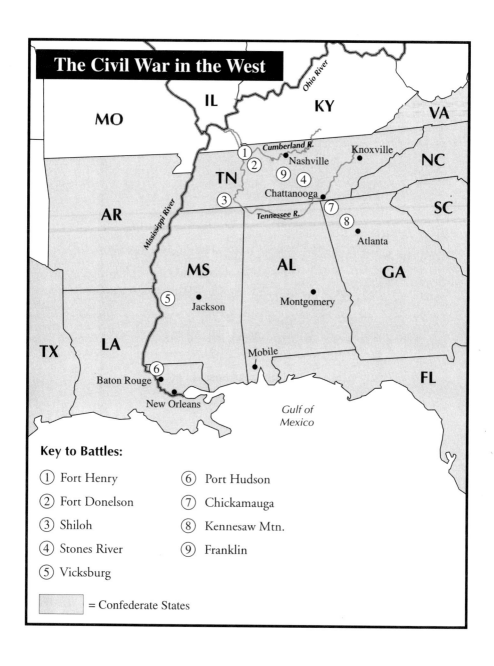

The Civil War in the West

Ohio River

MO

IL

KY

VA

NC

Cumberland R.

① Nashville

Knoxville

② TN

⑨ ④

③ Chattanooga

Tennessee R.

⑦

⑧

Atlanta

AR

Mississippi River

MS

AL

SC

GA

⑤ Jackson

Montgomery

TX

LA

Mobile

⑥

Baton Rouge

New Orleans

Gulf of Mexico

FL

Key to Battles:

① Fort Henry   ⑥ Port Hudson

② Fort Donelson   ⑦ Chickamauga

③ Shiloh   ⑧ Kennesaw Mtn.

④ Stones River   ⑨ Franklin

⑤ Vicksburg

▢ = Confederate States

in a few minutes the gallant Confederate commander bled to death. Still the Confederates pressed ahead, commanded now by General P. G. T. Beauregard.

Around 5:30 P.M., at the Hornets' Nest, Prentiss surrendered the 2,200 survivors of his nearly surrounded division. The Confederates had pushed the Yankees back two miles. As the sun set, the Union army appeared on the verge of total defeat. That night cold rain fell as artillery shells crashed among the trees. Union Brigadier General William Tecumseh Sherman found his commander huddled beneath a tree in the rain. "Well, Grant," he remarked, "we've had the devil's own day, haven't we?"

"Yes," quietly answered Grant, puffing hard on a cigar. "Yes. Lick 'em tomorrow, though."

Stubbornly General Grant planned a counterattack. During the night fresh Union regiments reached the battlefield. At dawn on April 7, the Yankees, now 50,000 strong, charged Beauregard's weary troops. The astonished Confederates fell back, firing as they went. By late afternoon, they gave up the battle completely, dropping guns and knapsacks as they ran.

By refusing to quit, the Union army had won the Battle of Shiloh. Many Northerners, however, gasped at the battle's bloody cost. In the two-day fight, as many as 13,000 Union and 11,000 Confederate soldiers had been killed, wounded, or captured. Shocked by the bloodshed, some Northern politicians demanded that Grant be relieved of duty. President Lincoln stood by his general, though. "I can't spare this man," Lincoln told Grant's critics. "He fights."

The Fight for Middle Tennessee

Union marines marched through the streets of New Orleans, Louisiana, on April 24, 1862. Union warships commanded by Flag Officer David G. Farragut had sailed up the Mississippi River and seized that busy port. By June, only one major river port remained in Confederate hands: Vicksburg, Mississippi. At the same time, the North still struggled to capture central Tennessee. "We move tomorrow, gentlemen!" Union Major General William Rosecrans told his generals on Christmas Day 1862. "Press them hard! Drive them out of their nests! Make them fight or run!"[3]

On December 30, Rosecrans's 44,000 marching Yankees neared a Confederate army of 33,000 men, commanded by General Braxton Bragg, camped along Stone's River near Murfreesboro, Tennessee. The two armies spent the night only a few hundred yards apart, their regimental bands competing with one another, alternating Northern and Southern tunes. Then a Federal band struck up "Home Sweet Home." Before long, Yankee and Rebel bands all along the battlelines were playing the lovely melody. "And after our bands had ceased playing," Yankee soldier W. J. Worsham recalled, "we could hear the sweet refrain as it died away on the cool frosty air."

The next morning the Union and Confederate armies attacked. Private R. B. Stewart recalled the charge of his Union regiment: "Our way was through [a] cornfield. . . . I could hear the bullets striking the stalks. I could hear them strike a comrade as he ran. Then there would be a groan, a stagger, and a fall . . ." Fighting furiously, the Rebels pressed their enemy backward. A Federal brigade commanded by Colonel William B. Hazen clung to its position in a thicket of cedar trees called the "Round Forest." With Colonel Julius P. Garesche riding close behind him, Rosecrans recklessly galloped forward to steady Hazen's men. Suddenly, a cannonball struck Garesche full in the face. The headless body, spouting blood, remained in the saddle for twenty paces before sliding to the ground.

As the day ended, freezing rain fell across the battlefield and onto the bloodied bodies of the wounded and dying. No major fighting occurred on New Year's Day 1863. But on the third day, January 2, 1863, Confederate General Bragg attacked again. In savage hand-to-hand fighting, the Rebels drove their enemy back to Stone's River. Supported by cannon, however, the Yankees fiercely counterattacked until the Southern ranks were smashed. That night in a drenching rain Bragg retreated southward with his surviving Rebels. Each side had suffered some 13,000 casualties in the brutal fighting. The Battle of Stone's River represented a major success for the North. But as Union Brigadier General Philip Sheridan admitted, "Our victory was dearly bought."

Vicksburg

"Vicksburg is the key," Abraham Lincoln declared. "The

war can never be brought to a close until the key is in our pocket." Lincoln assigned U. S. Grant the task of taking Vicksburg, Mississippi. By the end of January, 1863, Grant and 45,000 men of the U. S. Army of the Tennessee reached Young's Point, about ten miles upstream from that river city.

Through the next months Grant edged closer to Vicksburg's fortified river bluffs. Several times he showed his genius as he maneuvered for position and fought off Confederate attacks. If one effort failed, the stubborn general tried another. Union soldiers sank to their hips as they struggled through bayous and swamps. "This long, dreary . . . winter was one of great hardship to all engaged about Vicksburg," Grant later declared. "Troops could scarcely find dry ground on which to pitch their tents."[4]

Finally Grant decided on a daring plan. He would march down the western side of the river, cross below Vicksburg, and—without hope of resupply or reinforcement—come up from behind and take the town. On the night of April 16, Admiral David Dixon Porter's Union fleet steamed south directly past Vicksburg's cannon batteries. The fleet included three river transports carrying vital supplies. "It was as if hell itself were loose that night on the Mississippi River," Iowa Captain Samuel Byers recalled. Northern newsman Albert Richardson exclaimed, "The Mississippi bank was ablaze. Our [gunboats] promptly replied with their heaviest guns, while the transports, hugging the Louisiana shore, ran by as fast as possible."

The Federal army began ferrying across the Mississippi about fifty miles downriver from Vicksburg on April 30. Grant wrote later, "I was now in the enemy's country, with a river and the stronghold of Vicksburg between me and my base of supplies. But I was on dry ground on the same side of the river with the enemy."[5]

Grant's army slept on the ground at night and lived off the countryside by day. The general's only personal baggage consisted of a toothbrush. In the next three weeks, the Yankees marched 180 miles and beat the Confederates in five fights: at Port Gibson, Raymond, Jackson, Champion's Hill, and Big Black River. Finally the hardy Northerners surrounded Vicksburg, trapping some 31,000 Confederate soldiers within the city's defenses.

Three assaults failed before Grant decided "to outcamp" the enemy with a siege. Sweating Yankee soldiers dug rifle pits with picks and shovels. Others dragged artillery into position. "Every day," a Union private wrote, "the regiments, foot by foot, yard by yard, approached near the . . . rebel works. We got so we bored like gophers and beavers, with a spade in one hand and a gun in the other."

Union artillery bombarded the Confederates around the clock. Trapped inside Vicksburg, many Southern civilians and soldiers burrowed caves into the bluffs to escape the Union cannonfire. Some of the caves contained several rooms fitted out with rugs, beds, and chairs, and staffed with slaves. "We are utterly cut off from the world, surrounded by a circle of fire," a woman in Vicksburg bemoaned. "The fiery shower of shells goes on, day and night. . . . People do nothing but eat what they can get, sleep *when* they can, and dodge the shells."[6]

Food ran low among the city's defenders. They were reduced to eating mules, horses, and dogs. Even skinned rats hung in the windows of some butcher shops for sale. "If you can't feed us, you'd better surrender us," Confederate soldiers finally demanded in a letter to their commander. At last on July 3, 1863, Confederate General John Pemberton admitted defeat and surrendered his army. On July 4, 31,000 beaten Rebels marched out of Vicksburg and stacked their guns. Yankee soldiers raised the Stars and Stripes above the Vicksburg courthouse.

Bombproof shelters at Vicksburg, Mississippi. During the long siege Union soldiers dug these shelters in the side of a hill to protect themselves from enemy artillery shells. Confederate soldiers and civilians burrowed, too. "Caves were the fashion—the rage," remarked Vicksburg resident Mary Loughborough.

Grant's stunning victory at Vicksburg struck a terrific blow against the South. Five days later, a Confederate force at Port Hudson, Louisiana, also surrendered after a six-week siege. The Confederacy had been cut in two. Union soldiers and sailors now controlled the entire Mississippi River. "The Father of the Waters," Lincoln gratefully declared, "again goes unvexed to the sea."

*. . . if there is one man in either army ,
Confederate or Federal, head and shoulders
above every other . . . it is General Lee! . . . He
will take more desperate chances, and take them
quicker, than any other general in this country,
North or South.*

—Southern Colonel Joseph Ives, 1862

4 War in the East

Abraham Lincoln searched among the Union ranks for a general who could capture Richmond. At the same time, the Confederacy pinned its greatest hopes for victory on General Robert E. Lee.

Clash of the Ironclads

Four wooden Union warships stood at anchor in Hampton Roads, at the mouth of Virginia's James River on March 8, 1862. Suddenly Union sailor A. B. Smith aboard the U.S.S. *Cumberland,* noticed a strange vessel approaching. "As she came ploughing through the water . . . she looked like a huge, half-submerged crocodile," he exclaimed. Protected by iron plates bolted on its wooden hull, the Confederate warship *Merrimack* rammed and sank the *Cumberland* and smashed the U.S.S. *Congress* into a blazing wreck before darkness fell.

That night the first Union iron ship ever built also steamed into Hampton Roads. Designed by inventor John Ericsson, the *Monitor* possessed two guns mounted in a revolving turret. On March 9, 1862, the *Monitor* and the *Merrimack* hammered away at each other, hull to hull. The men inside, half-blind with smoke, loaded and fired, loaded and fired. "The shot, shell, grape, cannister, musket, and rifle balls flew about in every direction, but did us no damage," a Union lieutenant aboard the *Monitor* remembered.[1] After four and a half hours, the *Merrimack* broke off the fight, returning to its Norfolk,

The Union *Monitor* (left) and the Confederate *Merrimack* battle at Hampton Roads on March 9, 1862. Cannonballs striking the iron sides of the two ships seemed to have no more effect than "pebble-stones thrown by a child," exclaimed one astonished witness.

Virginia, port. Although a draw, the world's first duel between "ironclads" showed the power of iron warships over wooden ones. The navies of the world would never be the same.

New Commanders Take the Lead

After the Battle of Bull Run, thirty-four-year-old Major General George McClellan was appointed to command all Union troops in Washington. Second in his class at West Point, McClellan spent months drilling his Northern

Upon first seeing the *U.S.S. Monitor* one surprised Southerner said it looked like "an immense shingle floating on the water, with a gigantic cheese box rising from its center." Four months after its battle with the *Merrimack*, Union officers stand on the *Monitor's* deck. Dents in the turret's armor (at left) were made by the *Merrimack's* cannonballs.

volunteers and carefully building the new Union Army of the Potomac. A cautious military man, McClellan seemed to prefer parades and grand reviews rather than actual fighting. After long delays, McClellan at last ordered a landing on the Virginia coast. In April 1862, a great fleet of 400 vessels ferried his army of 120,000 to the neck of land between the York and the James Rivers. General Joseph Johnston commanded 60,000 Confederates in Virginia. At Yorktown and Williamsburg the Rebels slowed McClellan's advance. But day after day the Yankees inched through the mud closer to Richmond. By May 24, Union Sergeant Elisha Hunt Rhodes had written in his diary, "Richmond is just nine miles off. . . . From a hill nearby we can see the spires of the churches."[2]

For a time it seemed only Confederate Major General Thomas "Stonewall" Jackson saved Richmond from disaster. With just 16,000 fast-moving infantrymen, Jackson ranged up and down northern Virginia's Shenandoah Valley. Three Union commanders with a total of 64,000 troops could not defeat him. A deeply religious man, Jackson had his own special way of fighting. "Always mystify, mislead and surprise the enemy," he declared. During May and early June, Jackson scored victories at McDowell, Front Royal, Winchester, Cross Keys, and Port Republic. In Washington, Lincoln worried about Jackson's next move. Instead of sending additional Union troops to McClellan, he kept them nearby to protect the capital.

Finally on May 31, 1862, Confederate General Joseph Johnston attacked part of McClellan's army

J.E.B. Stuart (1833-1864) On his daring ride around McClellan's army, the Confederate cavalryman was chased unsuccessfully by Union troops commanded by his own father-in-law, Union Brigadier General Philip St. George Cooke. In 1864 Stuart would be fatally wounded in fighting at Yellow Tavern, Virginia.

outside of Richmond. In the heavy fighting at the Battle of Fair Oaks, Johnston fell severely wounded. Confederate President Jefferson Davis immediately named General Robert E. Lee to take command of the Confederate troops. The son of Revolutionary War hero "Light Horse Harry" Lee, fifty-four-year-old Robert E. Lee seemed the perfect soldier: West Point graduate, veteran of the Mexican War, former commandant of the U.S. Military Academy, and capturer of John Brown at Harper's Ferry. At the start of the war, Lincoln had offered Lee command of United States troops. But Lee, a Virginian, chose to stay loyal to Virginia.

Lee renamed his Confederate army the Army of Northern Virginia. Within days he sent his dashing young cavalry chief, Brigadier General J. E. B. Stuart, to scout McClellan's forces. On a thrilling three-day ride, Stuart circled around McClellan's entire army with 1,200 Rebel troopers. Joined by Stonewall Jackson's troops, Lee then attacked the Union enemy at Mechanicsville, Virginia on June 26, 1862.

Stunned by the attack, McClellan shifted his army southward. Fiercely, Lee pressed his advantage in bloody clashes at Gaines Mill, Savage's Station, and Frayser's Farm. At Malvern Hill, July 1, 1862, McClellan made a stand, massing 250 Federal cannon on the high slopes. Brashly Lee ordered waves of Confederates to attack. Confederate Major General D. H. Hill later exclaimed, "As each brigade emerged from the woods, from fifty to one hundred guns opened upon it, tearing great gaps in its ranks; but the heroes reeled on—and were shot

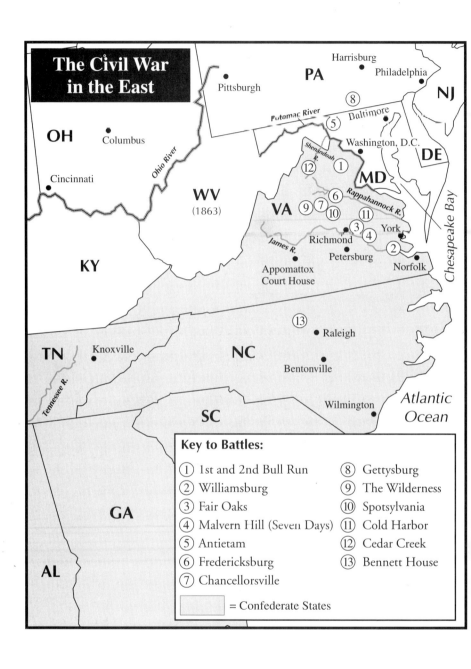

The Civil War in the East

Harrisburg

Philadelphia

PA

Pittsburgh

NJ

⑧

Potomac River

⑤ Baltimore

OH

Columbus

Washington, D.C.

DE

Ohio River

Shenandoah R.

MD

Cincinnati

⑫ ①

Rappahannock R.

WV
(1863)

VA

⑥

⑨ ⑦

⑩

⑪

York

③

④

KY

James R.

Richmond

Petersburg

②

Norfolk

Appomattox
Court House

Chesapeake Bay

⑬

Raleigh

TN

Knoxville

NC

Bentonville

Tennessee R.

Wilmington

**Atlantic
Ocean**

SC

GA

Key to Battles:

① 1st and 2nd Bull Run   ⑧ Gettysburg
② Williamsburg   ⑨ The Wilderness
③ Fair Oaks   ⑩ Spotsylvania
④ Malvern Hill (Seven Days)   ⑪ Cold Harbor
⑤ Antietam   ⑫ Cedar Creek
⑥ Fredericksburg   ⑬ Bennett House
⑦ Chancellorsville

☐ = Confederate States

AL

down. . . . It was not war—it was murder." That night McClellan withdrew his army to the safety of Harrison's Landing on the James River. Thus ended a week of almost constant fighting, the "Battles of the Seven Days." At a tremendous cost in lives, Lee had saved Richmond.

Without pause Lee started north to fight Major General John Pope, commander of the Union troops gathering in northern Virginia. On August 29, 1862, Pope clashed with Stonewall Jackson's corps near Manassas, site of the First Battle of Bull Run. When ammunition ran low some Rebels grabbed rocks and hurled them at the Yankees. The next day Lee sent Major General James Longstreet with 30,000 fresh Confederates storming into the exposed Union left flank. Virginia Private Alexander Hunter remembered: "A heavy volley on one side—a hurrah—a scream of rage. We got within ten yards of them—and they broke—and in a second they were running for the rear. Their guns were thrown away. They would unstrap their knapsacks as they ran—their hats would fly off—but nothing stopped them."

During this "Second Battle of Bull Run," 25,000 men were killed, wounded, or missing. The roads turned to mud in the rain as the shocked and exhausted Yankees trudged back toward Washington. Thus ended another campaign in which Lee and his ragged, ill-equipped, and outnumbered army had triumphed.

The Bloodiest Day

Full of confidence, on September 4, 1862, Lee marched

40,000 Confederate soldiers northward across the Potomac
River into Maryland. Lee guessed that the rich farmlands
of that border state would help keep his hungry Rebels fed.
He also wished to take the war into the North's territory.
To meet the emergency, Lincoln turned to General
McClellan again. With 100,000 Union troops, McClel-
lan marched north from Washington. Luck helped the
Yankees greatly. On September 13, in a meadow near
Frederick, Maryland, two Union soldiers found a lost
copy of Robert E. Lee's military plans. "Here is a paper
with which, if I cannot whip Bobbie Lee, I will be willing to go home," McClellan gleefully exclaimed.[3]

These Confederate dead lie where they fell along the Hagerstown
Turnpike. In the near distance to the right Union soldiers charged
through Miller's cornfield on September 17, 1862. The two
enemies "stood and shot one another," recalled one witness, "till the
lines melted away like wax."

Realizing his danger, Lee regrouped his army near the country town of Sharpsburg, Maryland, beside Antietam Creek. After wasting two full days bringing his Yankees into battle line, McClellan finally attacked at dawn on September 17, 1862.

North of Sharpsburg, Union troops charged into a thirty-acre cornfield owned by farmer D. R. Miller. Suddenly Confederate musket volleys whistled through the tall green cornstalks. "Men were knocked out of the ranks by dozens," Wisconsin Major Rufus Dawes later recalled. The Yankees fiercely pushed ahead to the Hagerstown Turnpike and past a simple white house of worship called the Dunker Church. Tough Texas soldiers furiously counterattacked, and fifteen times the battle surged back and forth across Miller's cornfield.

Late in the morning the fight shifted to a deeply rutted country path called the Sunken Road at the center of the Confederate defenseline. Rebels, crouched in this natural trench, watched a fresh Union division march toward them across open fields. "With all my lung power I shouted 'Fire!'" Alabama Colonel John B. Gordon later recalled. "Our rifles flamed and roared in the Federals' faces like a blinding blaze of lightning." Rows of Yankees fell, but in time the hard-pressed Confederate line broke. The retreating Confederates left dead comrades piled two and three deep in the place called ever afterwards "Bloody Lane."

Around 1:30 P.M. the battle shifted again, this time farther to the south. McClellan ordered Major General Ambrose Burnside to attack across Antietam Creek.

Burnside, with his bushy whiskers that set the style known as "sideburns," marched most of his 11,000 troops toward a sturdy stone bridge. Musketballs spit back and forth across the water, as the Yankees crossed the narrow span and swarmed up the bluffs beyond.

Retreating graycoats jammed the streets of Sharpsburg. Just when all seemed hopeless for the Rebels, Confederate Brigadier A. P. Hill and his Confederate "Light Division" arrived upon the field. Dressed in

Confederate dead on the Antietam battlefield. The Hagerstown Turnpike ran along behind the fence in the background. Farther away stands the simple Dunker Church where members of the German Baptist Brethren worshiped in more peaceful times.

After the Battle of Antietam, President Lincoln visited General
McClellan at his headquarters near Sharpsburg to discuss war plans.
Photographic negatives were made on square glass plates in those
days. This plate cracked, and as a result a line appears on the printed
photograph.

his bright red battle shirt, Hill ordered his 3,000 men to counterattack. As sunset neared, the charging Rebels fired rapid volleys and swept the surprised Yankees back to the bluffs along Antietam Creek. After twelve long hours, the Battle of Antietam ended, the bloodiest single day of the Civil War. In the woods and fields along Antietam Creek lay the crumpled corpses of 2,108 Union and 1,546 Confederate soldiers. The day's total number of killed, wounded, and missing men was more than 22,000.

On September 18, Lee's weary troops crossed the Potomac River and returned to Virginia. After a long summer of defeats, President Lincoln seized upon this moment of Union success to issue an important document. On September 22, he signed the Emancipation Proclamation. This presidential order proclaimed that beginning on January 1, 1863, "all persons held as slaves within any State . . . in rebellion against the United States, shall be then, henceforth, and forever free."[4] Before the Battle of Antietam, the North had fought only to hold the United States together. In the days ahead, however, the Union armies marched into battle knowing that the war would also abolish slavery.

Fredericksburg

Disappointed with McClellan's generalship, in November 1862 Lincoln gave Ambrose Burnside command of the Army of the Potomac. Burnside shifted 120,000 Yankees southward to the northern bank of the Rappahannock River. Across that river a line of hills overlooked Fredericksburg, Virginia. Lee stretched his 75,000 Rebels six and a half miles along the crests of the hills and awaited Burnside's attack.

On December 11, 1862, Yankee artillerymen fired 5,000 shells across the river into Fredericksburg. The explosions tore gaping holes in brick houses, set wooden houses ablaze, and dug craters in streets. Boatloads of Union troops soon rowed over and cleared the battered town of Rebel sharpshooters. At the same time Yankee engineers built pontoon bridges across the water. On December 13, under cover of a morning fog, the massive Union advance began. Thousands of bluecoats marched across the pontoon bridges and attacked. The main assault force under Union Major General Joseph Hooker was ordered to take Marye's Heights, heavily defended by Confederate artillery. A four-foot-high stone wall ran along the bottom of the hill. Behind it, four lines of Rebel infantry stood ready to pour steady rifle volleys on those Yankees who survived the cannonfire.

Louisiana artilleryman William Owen watched from Marye's Heights as the Union line advanced toward his guns: "How beautifully they came on! Their bright bayonets glistening in the sunlight made the line look like a huge serpent of blue and steel. . . . We could see our shells bursting in their ranks, making great gaps; but on they came, as though they would go straight through us and over us."[5]

Fourteen assaults were beaten back from Marye's Heights before Burnside realized the position could not be taken. Over 7,000 courageous Yankees fell under the

Confederate guns. Not a single Union soldier reached the stone wall. Lee watched the gallant charges from the heights above and said, "It is well that war is so terrible; otherwise we should grow too fond of it."

That freezing night the Confederates behind the stone wall could hear the wounded Yankees groaning and calling for water. One brave South Carolina Rebel loaded himself with canteens. Sergeant Richard Kirkland spent hours the next day tending to the wounded lying on the cold, muddy ground between the battle lines. Saluted by both sides as the "Angel of Marye's Heights," Kirkland himself would die in battle nine months later.

Altogether at Fredericksburg, the Union lost 12,600 men. The Confederates lost 5,300. On the night of December 15, the Yankees withdrew from the battlefield. Under cover of a driving rainstorm, the whole army recrossed the Rappahannock. In their old camps the heartsick Yankees settled down into winter quarters.

Lee's Boldest Stroke

With the failure of Burnside, Lincoln assigned yet another general to head the Army of the Potomac. In April 1863 Major General Joseph Hooker marched 70,000 Yankees across the Rappahannock River. "Fighting Joe" planned to outflank Lee and hit the Confederates from the rear. In swift response, Lee left just 10,000 men to defend Fredericksburg and rushed his remaining 50,000 troops west to meet Hooker's main attack.

Within a dense forest known as the Wilderness the two armies clashed at a country crossroads called

Chancellorsville on May 1. Everything seemed to be in Hooker's favor during that first day's fighting. That evening in the forest south of Chancellorsville Confederate staff officer James Power Smith observed a historic meeting. "I saw, bending over a scant fire of twigs, two men seated on old cracker boxes and warming their hands over the little fire. I had but to rub my eyes and collect my wits to recognize the figures of Robert E. Lee and Stonewall Jackson."

During that meeting Jackson proposed a daring gamble. With the Army of Northern Virginia heavily outnumbered and already divided, he suggested leaving only 20,000 men with Lee to face Hooker's 70,000 head-on. Jackson would take 30,000 men twelve miles through the woods and smash Hooker's exposed right flank. "Well," Lee boldly agreed, "go on."

Guided by a local civilian who knew the way through the woods, Jackson spent May 2 marching around Hooker's lines. About sundown, Union Private Warren Goss later recalled, "the soldiers of the Eleventh Corps, with stacked arms, were boiling their coffee, smoking their pipes, lounging in groups, and playing cards . . . when . . . Jackson's men . . . burst upon them like a clap of thunder from a cloudless sky."[6] The shocked Federals fell back two miles before Union artillery and nightfall halted the Confederate sweep.

Eager to continue the fight, Jackson and several of his officers rode out to scout the enemy lines. As they returned in the darkness, soldiers of the 18th North Carolina Regiment mistook them for Union cavalry and

Confederate General Robert E. Lee (1807-1870) In battle, his Army of Northern Virginia was almost always outnumbered by the Union enemy. Lee realized he had to take daring chances in order to win victories.

opened fire. Two of Jackson's aides fell dead from their saddles. Jackson himself was hit, one bullet striking his right hand and two more smashing into his left arm. Soldiers carried him to a field hospital where surgeons amputated his shattered arm the next morning.

Hard fighting on May 3 forced the Yankees farther backward. On May 6, the Union army retreated back across the Rappahannock. Hooker had lost 17,000 men. For Lee, it had been a brilliant but costly victory. Some 13,000 Confederates lay dead or wounded. But it was the loss of one man that concerned Lee most. After the amputation of his arm, Stonewall Jackson had been moved to a farmhouse at nearby Guiney's Station. There Lee's most valued general developed pneumonia and fever. Just before his death on May 10, Jackson muttered, "Let us cross over the river and rest under the shade of the trees."

The Turning Point

"My God! My God! What will the country say?" exclaimed Abraham Lincoln when he learned of Hooker's defeat at Chancellorsville. On June 28, Lincoln named General George G. Meade new commander of the Army of the Potomac. Already 75,000 lean Confederate soldiers tramped along the dirt and gravel roads leading through Maryland into Pennsylvania. Once more Robert E. Lee hoped to win complete Confederate victory by invading the North.

Confederate Major General Henry Heth needed shoes for the barefoot soldiers in his division. So he

Thomas "Stonewall" Jackson (1824-1863) Jackson posed for this
photograph two weeks before the Battle of Chancellorsville. When
he learned of the wounding of his most valued officer, General Lee
declared, "He has lost his left arm, but I have lost my right."

ordered his men to march to the town of Gettysburg, Pennsylvania, which was said to have a shoe factory. On the morning of July 1, 1863, Heth's soldiers advanced along the Chambersburg Turnpike. Suddenly gunshots rang out. Patrolling Union cavalrymen crouched in the woods ahead. Neither side had planned to fight at Gettysburg. But as Union and Confederate regiments reached the town, they bravely charged into the developing fight.

By the morning of July 2, 65,000 Confederates faced 85,000 Union troops defending the heights south of the town. Stretching over three miles, the Union defense line looked like a giant fishhook. Culp's Hill formed the point of the hook. It curved around and joined Cemetery Hill, Cemetery Ridge, and finally two high rocky hills called Little Round Top and Big Round Top. "Gentlemen, we will attack," Robert E. Lee told his

Gettysburg, Pennsylvania. Like spokes on a wheel, many roads led into Gettysburg, making battle there possible. Culp's Hill, Cemetery Hill, and rising Cemetery Ridge stand just south of the town.

Confederate generals. That afternoon Major General James Longstreet sent 12,000 Southern troops charging toward the Round Tops and Cemetery Ridge.

"Forward men, to the ledge!" exclaimed Confederate Colonel William C. Oates at the head of two attacking Alabama regiments. Rifles blazing, the Rebels surged upward over the rocky ground of Little Round Top. Only 380 men of the 20th Maine Regiment defended this position. Muskets flashed as the thin Yankee line wavered back and forth. "Fix bayonets," shouted Union Colonel

A Confederate sharpshooter lies dead among the maze of rocks and boulders called the "Devil's Den."

Joshua Chamberlain when the Yankees' ammunition was gone. "Charge!" Yelling wildly, the Maine men finally drove the Alabama troops off of the hill.

Below Little Round Top other Rebel regiments charged among the great boulders of a place local farmers called the "Devil's Den." "Here they come! Here they come!" shouted the Yankee defenders as the Rebels ran forward. Smoke and rifle-fire rolled through the stones. Farther to the north, in front of Cemetery Ridge, the Rebels rushed into a wheatfield and a peach orchard. Bullets smacked into bodies, and Union cannonfire blasted among the peach trees. Hundreds of Rebel troops dropped to the ground dead and wounded.

Longstreet's attacks on July 2 failed to break the Union line. That night General Lee planned a final attack. Major General George Pickett's division of Virginians would go into battle the next day with three other divisions and strike the center of the Union line on Cemetery Ridge. The Rebels opened the attack on July 3 with a tremendous barrage of artillery-fire. Howling shells burst among the Yankees and cannonballs tore furrows in the ground. Pennsylvania citizens living 140 miles away later claimed they heard the awful noise. "Charge the enemy and remember old Virginia!" General Pickett at last shouted to his men. Rank after rank of Confederate soldiers, 15,000 men altogether, marched forward beneath the July sun and started up the slope. Union cannonshells crashed into the advancing gray lines. Near the crest of the ridge, the Rebels charged toward a crooked angle in a low stone wall.

Three Confederate soldiers captured during the Battle of Gettysburg. Rebels such as these fought with fury to the very end.

"Who will follow me?" shouted Confederate Brigadier General Lewis A. Armistead. With his hat stuck on the tip of his upraised sword for all his men to see, Armistead leaped over the stone wall. Yankee bullets soon knocked him to the ground. "Men fire into each other's faces, not five feet apart," exclaimed witness Charles Coffin. "There are bayonet thrusts, saber strokes, pistol shots . . . hand-to-hand contests." For a few frightful minutes the battle wavered back and forth. But at last the Union line held. The Confederate survivors staggered back down the ridge and across the valley.

During Pickett's Charge 6,500 Confederates had fallen or been captured. "It has been a sad, sad day to us," admitted General Lee. "We must now return to Virginia." Together with the surrender of Vicksburg on July 4, the Battle of Gettysburg gave the Yankees a double victory. "The charm of Robert Lee . . . is broken," joyfully exclaimed New Yorker George Templeton Strong. After years of defeats, the Union Army of the Potomac had finally shown what it could do. The three-day fight at Gettysburg would be the bloodiest battle of the Civil War, with nearly 50,000 men killed, wounded, or missing. It also marked a turning point. At Gettysburg, Lee had gambled and failed.

When Johnny comes marching home again,
Hurrah! Hurrah!
We'll give him a hardy welcome then,
Hurrah! Hurrah!
The men will cheer, and the boys will shout;
The ladies they will all turn out, And we'll
all feel gay, When Johnny comes marching home.

—from an 1863 song written by Patrick Sarsfield Gilmore

5 Behind the Lines

American citizens in the North and the South carefully watched the progress of the fighting. The hand of war often reached beyond the major battlefields to touch the lives of men and women, young and old, behind the battlelines.

Filling the Ranks

Patriotic volunteers lined up at Northern and Southern army recruiting offices at the war's start. The Union army paid enlisted soldiers $13 a month, the Confederate army $11. Starting in 1862 the U.S. government offered an extra $100 bounty to volunteers. Many Northern states paid additional enlistment bonuses. Some crafty "bounty jumpers" enlisted, collected their money, then deserted, only to join again in other states. Thousands of new immigrants joined Yankee regiments, including some 200,000 Germans and 150,000 Irishmen. Native Americans also served in the Confederate and Union armies. General Grant's military secretary, Eli Parker, for example, was a full-blooded Senaca Indian.

As the war dragged on, it became more difficult to find volunteers. In April 1862, the Confederate Congress passed America's first draft law, drafting men between the ages of eighteen and thirty-five years. Lincoln issued a draft call in the summer of 1863, requesting 300,000 fresh Union troops. Any drafted man who paid a $300 fee or found a substitute willing to serve in his place, could stay at home. Future U. S. presidents Chester A. Arthur and Grover Cleveland, for example, both paid for substitutes.

Drafted Southerners unable to pay for substitutes complained about "the rich man's war and the poor man's fight." Many poor Northerners also resented the draft. On July 13, 1863, an angry mob burned New York City's draft office. The frenzied crowd then looted nearby houses and shops. One stunned New York woman watched the rioters race through the streets: "Thousands . . . yelling, screaming and swearing . . . like a company of raging fiends."[1] Policemen and ex-soldiers battled the wild throngs until troops fresh from the battlefield of Gettysburg finally arrived to restore order. As many as 119 people were killed during four days of bloody riots.

On July 18, just three days after the New York City draft riots ended, the Negro 54th Massachusetts

Taylor, a Union drummer boy. Some two hundred thousand African Americans bravely answered the North's call to arms and served in the United States military during the Civil War.

Regiment assaulted Confederate Fort Wagner on the coast of South Carolina with heavy losses. The U.S. Congress first authorized African-American recruitment in 1862. "They will make good soldiers," General U. S. Grant predicted. Altogether 180,000 African Americans wore the Union army's blue uniform. Another 20,000 African Americans served in the U.S. Navy. African Americans fought and died at Port Hudson, Louisiana; Milliken's Bend, Louisiana; Fort Wagner, South Carolina; and on dozens of other battlefields. By war's end twenty-one African-American soldiers and sailors had won the Congressional Medal of Honor for bravery.

The Soldier's Life

"The first thing in the morning is drill. Then drill, then drill again. Then drill, drill, a little more drill. Then drill, and lastly drill." So wrote Pennsylvania Private Oliver Norton of his first taste of army life. In camp new officers thumbed through copies of *Hardee's Rifle and Light Infantry Tactics* to learn training regulations. Sergeants barked orders as they taught enlisted men the correct methods of marching and handling a musket. The invention of new weapons made killing during the Civil War easier and more terrible than ever before. Frenchman Claude Minié had introduced a new bullet in 1842. Spinning out of the grooved barrel of a rifled musket, a "minié ball" could kill at a distance of a half mile. Gunsmith Samuel Colt manufactured repeating pistols and rifles in his Hartford, Connecticut, factory. Northerner

Christopher Spencer invented a repeating rifle that could fire seven cartridges within a few seconds.

Although rifle bullets caused three-quarters of battlefield casualties, artillery also proved to be very deadly. Field guns drawn by horses followed infantrymen on the march. Their wheeled caissons, or ammunition boxes, contained three common types of ammunition: solid cannonballs, exploding metal shells, and canisters that sprayed out pellets like giant shotgun blasts. Depending on its design, size, and ammunition, a field cannon could fire distances as far away as 5,000 yards.

For a uniform, a typical Union infantry private wore a blue cap, blue coat, blue woolen trousers, and simple leather shoes. His weapon was usually a Springfield rifle. Atop his knapsack he often tied his rolled wool blanket. Inside the pack he carried half of a two-man "dog tent," a square of oilcloth used to keep the floor of his tent dry, and an overcoat. Personal items might include spare socks; a clean shirt; a tin plate, cup, knife, fork, and spoon; a sewing kit commonly called a "housewife"; a razor, mirror, and comb; and a pipe and tobacco. A fully equipped Union soldier carried fifty pounds on his back.

A typical Confederate soldier wore a soft felt "slouch" hat of gray or "butternut" brown, and a homespun uniform of the same color. Instead of a heavy knapsack he rolled his personal items into his blankets, which he slung over his shoulder. His weapon was either the Springfield rifle or a British-made Enfield rifle. Dangling from his belt was a cartridge box large enough to hold

These proud Confederates of 1861 show off their handsome
uniforms. As the war progressed, such fancy clothes were seen
less often among the poorly supplied Rebel ranks. The flat cap
with the stiff brim is called a "kepi" from a design made popular
in the French military.

forty rounds of ammunition, a bayonet, a canteen, and a tin cup. Often he used gear captured from the enemy.

Union quartermasters fed Yankee troops corn meal, beans, bacon, pickled beef—called "salt horse"—and always a hard, square biscuit called "hardtack." Confederate troops often ate "sloosh," cornmeal swirled in bacon grease, then wrapped around a ramrod and cooked over the campfire.

Soldiers made their long winter encampments as comfortable as possible. In winter camps Union soldiers often built regular huts of wood with wooden barrels for chimneys. Rebel soldiers threw together "shebangs," crude shelters made of pine branches and oilcloths. The idle troops read newspapers, magazines, and books. Many homesick soldiers wrote letters, while others kept diaries. For entertainment, soldiers wrestled, held boxing matches, ran races, and played baseball. Around campfires at night, the armies sang such sentimental songs as "Lorena," "The Vacant Chair," "Tenting Tonight," "All Quiet Along the Potomac," and "When This Cruel War Is Over." "Dixie" became the unofficial anthem of the Confederacy, while "The Battle Hymn of the Republic," written by Julia Ward Howe, thrilled Union soldiers.

Guerrilla Fighters and Cavalry Raiders

"Kill every man big enough to carry a gun," the commander coldly instructed his raiders. Along the Missouri-Kansas border, Yankee and Rebel guerrillas fought a brutal war. The best-known Missouri guerrilla was Rebel William Clarke Quantrill, quoted above.

Gathering together a bunch of wild "bushwhackers," including future train robbers Frank and Jesse James, Quantrill rampaged through the border countryside.

The worst of Quantrill's raids occurred in Lawrence, Kansas, on August 21, 1863. While Quantrill calmly ate breakfast in a Lawrence hotel, his men shot down unarmed citizens and set fire to the town. Rising from his cellar hiding place afterwards, the stunned Reverend H. D. Fisher discovered that "more than one hundred and eighty of our citizens had been killed and . . . the whole business part of our town was in ashes." Quantrill caused mayhem in Missouri, Kansas, and Texas until he was finally killed during a clash with Union troops in May 1865.

In Virginia, Confederate Colonel John S. Mosby led irregular cavalrymen into Fairfax Court House on March 9, 1863. There he captured thirty-three Union soldiers, including Brigadier General Edwin Stoughton. Fighting behind the Union lines, Mosby and his men tore up rail lines, blew up bridges, robbed trains, and attacked Union supply wagons and cavalry patrols. "Mosby is continually around us," complained Union Colonel Henry Gansevoort. Though "Mosby's Rangers" seldom numbered more than 200, they caused more trouble for the Yankees than any other guerrilla group.

Regular cavalry units also attacked the enemy behind their lines. A slave trader before the war, Nathan Bedford Forrest became the most successful cavalry commander in the Confederate service, rising from the rank of private to lieutenant general. He was a master of the lightning raid.

At Brice's Cross Roads near Tupelo, Mississippi, Forrest's 8,000 cavalrymen defeated a Union force twice its size in June 1864. Time and time again Forrest cut the Union supply line in Tennessee by attacking railroad outposts, tearing up rails, and burning bridges.

In April 1863, General U. S. Grant ordered Union Colonel Benjamin Grierson to lead one of the most daring cavalry raids of the war. On April 17, at the head of 1,700 Iowa and Illinois horsemen, Grierson rode southward from La Grange, Tennessee, deep into the heart of enemy territory in Mississippi. As many as 20,000 Confederate troops tried to capture the Yankee raiders. But Grierson avoided their traps and stayed ahead of them. On May 2, 1863, Grierson's raiders finished their amazing 600-mile ride and reached the safety of the Union lines at Baton Rouge, Louisiana. Grierson later reported that his men "killed and wounded about one hundred of the enemy, captured . . . over 500 prisoners . . . destroyed between fifty and sixty miles of railroad and . . . also captured 1,000 horses and mules."[2] By keeping the Confederates in Mississippi occupied during two important weeks, Grierson helped make Grant's siege of Vicksburg possible.

Nurses and Hospitals

"Almost every house in the city was a private hospital, and almost every woman a nurse," reported Sallie Brock of Richmond in June 1862, after the bloody Battle of Fair Oaks. Before each battle it was the duty of the regimental surgeon to select a site for his field hospital about

A Union hospital near Washington, D.C. "The military hospitals . . . in Washington and its neighborhood," wrote New York poet and nurse Walt Whitman in 1863, "sometimes contain over fifty thousand sick and wounded men. Every form of wound . . . every kind of malady."

two miles to the rear. Lieutenant W. W. Blackford after
First Bull Run passed one Confederate field hospital:
"Tables about breast high had been erected upon which
screaming victims were having legs and arms cut off. The
surgeons and their assistants, stripped to the waist and
bespattered with blood, stood around, some holding the
poor fellows while others, armed with long, bloody knives
and saws, cut and sawed away . . . throwing the mangled
limbs on a pile nearby as soon as removed."[3]

Army nursing was considered a man's job. New York
poet Walt Whitman became a nurse in Washington hospitals after his brother was wounded at Antietam. Clara
Barton was one of the first female nurses. She first arrived on a battlefield after the Battle of Cedar Mountain
in Virginia on August 9, 1862. Union army doctor
James I. Dunn reported: "While the shells were bursting
in every direction . . . she [stayed] dealing out shirts to
the naked wounded, and preparing soup and seeing it
prepared in all the hospitals." At Antietam,
Fredericksburg, and elsewhere, Barton braved the gunfire
to aid the wounded until she became famous throughout
the North as the "Angel of the Battlefield." After the
war, in 1882, Clara Barton founded the American Red
Cross to provide aid to disaster victims.

The U.S. Sanitary Commission distributed food,
clothes, and medicines to needy Union soldiers. Ohio
widow Mary Ann Bickerdyke, a Sanitary Commission
agent, traveled with the Union armies in the west
through four years and nineteen battles, nursing the
grateful men, who called her "Mother Bickerdyke." By

war's end more than 3,000 Northern women served as regular army nurses. They worked under the strict direction of Superintendent Dorothea Dix. Southern women worked as nurses, too. Sally Tompkins with a staff of six nursed 1,333 wounded men in her private Richmond hospital.

Of all the hospitals in the North and South the biggest and best was Chimborazo at Richmond, with its 8,000 beds, five soup kitchens, a dairy, a brewery, and a bakery that turned out 10,000 loaves of bread a day. Chimborazo nurse Phoebe Yates Pember later remembered, "I bring comfort, strength and I believe happiness to many sick beds daily and lie down at night with a happy consciousness of time well and unselfishly spent.[4]

Prisons North and South

"It is useless to attempt a description of the place," declared an Alabama prisoner at Fort Delaware, Delaware. "A respectable hog would have turned up his nose in disgust of it." Thousands of soldiers captured in battle spent harsh months in prison. Altogether some 150 different places were used as prisons in the North and South. Most were overcrowded and filthy. Although Camp Morton near Indianapolis, Indiana, was one of the best-run prison camps, more than 1,700 Confederate soldiers died there. Smallpox killed 1,800 Rebel prisoners at Rock Island, Illinois.

Rebel prisoners were often fed skimpy rations of coffee, soup, and bread. An Arkansas soldier imprisoned at Johnson's Island on Lake Erie later wrote, "We trapped

The prison at Andersonville, Georgia. As many as 33,000 Union prisoners were crowded inside without wooden shelters, medicine, or a clean water supply. "One could not look a rod in any direction," recalled prisoner John McElroy, "without seeing at least a dozen men in the last frightful stages of rotting Death."

for rats and the prisoners [ate] every one they could get. . . . They was all right to a hungry man." Nearly 9,600 Confederate soldiers were jammed into prison barracks built to house half that many at Elmira, New York. There were never enough blankets for all the Rebels. A survivor recalled, "Each morning the men crawled out of their bunks shivering and half-frozen." During the winter of 1864 Elmira prisoners died of cold and sickness at the rate of ten a day.

Yankees suffered just as much in Confederate prisons. Libby Prison in Richmond was a converted three-story tobacco warehouse. Six dank rooms housed 1,300 Union officers. Belle Isle on the James River crammed thousands of enlisted Yankees into a large open pen. "On Saturday night four or five of our soldiers froze to death on Belle Isle!" wrote imprisoned Union General Neal Dow in his diary on January 4, 1864.[5]

The worst prison of all was Andersonville in Georgia, a stockade of twenty-seven acres surrounded by high pine walls. Opened in early 1864 and meant for 10,000 Union prisoners, it held 33,000 by August. Forbidden to build shelters, the men scratched holes into the ground and covered them with blankets. A line of wooden posts stood fifteen feet inside the stockade. Any man crossing this "deadline" was shot down. New York Private A. S. Clyne later declared, "When I was taken prisoner I weighed 165 pounds, and when I came out I weighed 96 pounds, and was considered stout compared with some I saw there." Altogether, disease and starvation killed 13,000 men at Andersonville.

Lincoln the Statesman and Politician

"I laugh," Lincoln told a friend during the darkest days of the war, "because I must not cry." Gloomy reports of Union defeats and deaths on the battlefields greatly saddened Lincoln. He often haunted the War Department telegraph office, hoping for good news. Faithful Northerners called him "Father Abraham," and at times it seemed the nation's fate rested on Lincoln's shoulders alone. To relieve the pressure, Lincoln sometimes cracked jokes in the White House.

Enemies called Lincoln an ape, a baboon, and a fool. In his letters and speeches, however, the sixteenth U.S. president showed his true genius. On November 19,

Soldiers and civilians crowd close to hear Lincoln speak at Gettysburg. Lincoln is seated on the speaker's platform (in front of the tree) and has not yet risen to give his address.

Abraham Lincoln (1809-1865) Worn down by two years of civil war the weary sixteenth U.S. president posed for this photograph on November 8, 1863. Eleven days later he spoke immortal words at Gettysburg, Pennsylvania.

1863, Lincoln spoke at the dedication of a National Cemetery at Gettysburg. In his brief "Gettysburg Address" Lincoln began, "Fourscore and seven years ago our fathers brought forth on this continent a new nation, conceived in liberty, and dedicated to the proposition that all men are created equal." He called upon his listeners to continue the fight so that "government of the people, by the people, for the people, shall not perish from the earth."[6]

Above all things, Lincoln wished to see the war ended and the United States reunited. Some Northerners, however, desired peace at any price. Antiwar Democrats called "Copperheads" demanded the political defeat of Lincoln and his policies. In the midst of a bloody civil war, the United States held a presidential election in 1864. The Democrats nominated George McClellan to run for president. They paraded in the streets singing, "O General McClellan, he is the man. He licked the Rebels at Antietam." The Republicans nominated Lincoln to a second term. A newspaperman for the London *Daily News* saw how deeply many Northerners loved Lincoln: "His jokes, his plain common sense, his shrewdness . . . and straight-forwardness, go right to their hearts," he reported.

Most Union soldiers supported "Honest Abe." Union victories in the fall of 1864 gave Northerners hope that perhaps the war could be won after all. On November 8, 1864, Lincoln won the election with 55 percent of the vote. The North had decided he was the man to see the war to its proper end.

I wonder what the South thinks of us Yankees now! I think Gettysburg will cure the Rebels of any desire to invade the North again.
—Union soldier Elisha Hunt Rhodes, July 4, 1863

6 When This Cruel War Is Over

Even after the Battle of Gettysburg, Confederates clung to the hope that if they prolonged their resistance, the North might yet grow utterly sick of the war and let the South go.

River of Death

Just south of the Tennessee border a little stream twisted through the Georgia woods and meadows. When the Cherokee Indians lived in the region they named the creek the Chickamauga, the River of Death. Since the Battle of Stone's River, Union General William Rosecrans and Confederate General Braxton Bragg had maneuvered for position until at last their armies faced one another along the Chickamauga.

The rattle of rifles and the roar of artillery echoed

over the water on the morning of September 19, 1863. In the bloody fighting at Chickamauga, Confederate cavalry officer Colonel Thomas Berry saw, "The ghastly, mangled dead and horribly wounded strewed . . . for over half a mile up and down the river banks." The battlelines swayed back and forth until darkness fell. The next day confused orders allowed a wide gap to open in the Yankee lines. Entirely by chance, General James Longstreet sent three Confederate divisions charging forward at that moment. Nearly 23,000 Rebel troops stormed across the fields and poured through the hole. "I saw our lines break and melt away like leaves before the wind," declared War Department official Charles Dana.[1] Men, horses, mules, ambulances, baggage wagons, ammunition wagons, artillery carriages, and caissons tumbled together in confused retreat.

The left side of the Union line refused to give up the fight, however. On a rise known as Snodgrass Hill, Major General George Thomas shouted orders to his troops. Through the day his men beat back twenty-five Rebel attacks. At nightfall, these brave Yankees retreated in good order. The two-day battle was over. Thomas's tough stand saved the Union army from complete defeat and earned him the lasting nickname of the "Rock of Chickamauga." At Chattanooga, Tennessee, General William Rosecrans began to reorganize his shaken army.

Missionary Ridge

On October 22, 1863, General U. S. Grant crossed the Tennessee River into Chattanooga to take command of

General Rosecrans' troops. To the south, General Bragg's Confederate army now occupied the long crest of Missionary Ridge and the two-thousand-foot summit of Lookout Mountain. Poised upon these heights, Bragg's Rebels confidently gazed down upon the penned-up Union army.

Instead of waiting for defeat, on November 24, Grant ordered an attack on Lookout Mountain. General Joseph Hooker with 10,000 Yankees charged up the rocky ledges. "We could plainly see Hooker's troops driving the Confederates up the face of the mountain," declared Union Brigadier General Philip Sheridan. "About this time . . . a cloud settled down on the mountain, and a

"The Battle Above the Clouds." Three Yankee divisions commanded by Major General Joseph Hooker stormed and captured Lookout Mountain on November 24, 1863.

heavy bank of fog obscured its whole face." The fight on Lookout Mountain became known as "The Battle Above the Clouds." By the end of the day the U.S. flag waved from the summit. The right side of the Union battleline was secure.

On November 25, Grant ordered General Thomas to capture the Confederate rifle pits at the foot of Missionary Ridge and then await further orders. Seated on horseback Grant watched 20,000 Union troops gallantly charge across the open ground. Muskets cracked and gunsmoke rose in choking clouds as the Yankees rushed ahead. At the foot of Missionary Ridge they captured the Confederate rifle pits. Then without pause they scrambled up the slope. "Who ordered those men up the hill?" Grant asked in startled anger.

Union staff officer Henry Cist later recalled, "Without further waiting . . . the entire line . . . advanced over and around rocks, under and through the fallen timber, [and] charged up the ridge." Eighteen-year-old Lieutenant Arthur MacArthur, Jr., of the 24th Wisconsin, carried his unit's colors to the top shouting, "On, Wisconsin," in the face of deadly gunfire. MacArthur won the Medal of Honor for his heroic deed. In World War II his son, General Douglas MacArthur, would also win a Medal of Honor.

As the yelling Yankees clambered upward, sudden fear gripped the Rebels. "A panic which I never before witnessed seemed to have seized upon officers and men," General Bragg later exclaimed.[2] Thousands of Rebels tried to escape. "Gray-clad men rushed wildly down the hill and into the woods, tossing away knapsacks, muskets, and blankets as they ran," declared one gleeful Yankee. The charge up Missionary Ridge had proven a complete triumph. Not only had Grant saved Chattanooga but, he had routed the Confederate army. Some 4,000 Confederate prisoners were taken on Missionary Ridge, as Bragg's army retreated into Georgia.

Battling for Atlanta

"War is cruelty. There is no use trying to reform it; the crueler it is, the sooner it will be over," remarked Union Major General William T. Sherman. Called east to greater duty, Grant left Sherman in command of the Union army at Chattanooga. Sherman's orders were to seize Atlanta, the "Gate City of the South" and an important Confederate manufacturing center. On May 6, 1864, the 98,000 men of Sherman's Grand Army of the West marched south into Georgia.

General Joseph E. Johnston returned to duty to take Bragg's place in command of the Confederate army in Georgia. Outgunned, outsupplied, outnumbered almost two to one, Johnston could only hope to slow Sherman's advance. In fighting at Dalton, Resaca, Cassville, and New Hope Church, Sherman forced the Rebels southward. By the end of June, Sherman found Johnston's men dug in across the face of Kennesaw Mountain, just twenty miles north of Atlanta. Impatiently, Sherman attacked the enemy head on. On June 27, 13,000 Union men stormed up Kennesaw Mountain. "The wonder was that any lived through such a storm

Confederate defenses at Atlanta, Georgia in the summer of 1864. The Rebels stripped boards from the houses in the background and built trench walls with them. Sharpened sticks inserted in tree trunks formed strong barricades called "chevaux-de-frise."

of shot and shell . . . and canister and musket balls," declared Ohio Major James T. Holmes. "It was a costly experiment."[3] After losing 3,000 men, Sherman grimly returned to safer fighting tactics.

Already Johnston had surrendered too much Georgia soil to suit Confederate President Jefferson Davis. On July 17, Davis replaced Johnston with thirty-three-year-old Lieutenant General John Bell Hood of Kentucky. The mangled arm Hood had suffered at Gettysburg and the leg he had lost at Chickamauga proved he was a fighting general. On July 20, 1864, Hood hit Sherman hard at Peachtree Creek, just north of Atlanta, but without success. Fierce attacks at Decatur and at Ezra Church also failed to drive away the Yankees. In just ten days of fighting Hood lost a third of his army—18,000 men. Defensively he fell back to Atlanta.

Swiftly, Sherman surrounded the city from the north, east, and west. Federal guns began shelling the Confederate trenches and the city beyond. The siege went on for a month. On August 9, Federal gunners poured more than 5,000 shells into the city. On that day at least six civilians, including women and children, died in the bombardment. Finally Sherman boldly marched south with 60,000 of his men. On August 31, he hurled these troops toward Jonesboro to cut the last Confederate railroad line leading into Atlanta. Hood realized he could hold the city no longer. Tearful citizens watched Hood's soldiers march away in retreat on September 1. The next day Yankee troops strode through the streets.

"Atlanta is ours and fairly won," Sherman telegraphed north to Washington.

If It Takes All Summer

"Grant don't care a snap if men fall like the leaves fall," wrote Southerner Mary Chesnut in her diary. "He fights to win, that chap does." Promoted to lieutenant general, U. S. Grant received command of all Union armies in March of 1864. While Sherman battled in Georgia, Grant chose to travel with the 110,000 men of the Army of the Potomac in Virginia.

General Robert E. Lee's 60,000 Confederate soldiers grimly waited for the Union attack. It began on May 5, 1864, in the tangled Virginia forest known as the Wilderness. Union Private Theodore Garrish remembered, "The rebels fought like demons, and under cover of the dense underbrush poured deadly volleys upon us. . . . Minié bullets went snapping and tearing . . . and the air was loaded with death."[4] Parts of the woods caught fire, and dozens of wounded men, too badly hurt to escape, burned to death.

The two-day Battle of the Wilderness ended in bloody stalemate. Although Grant lost 17,000 men, instead of retreating he shifted his army southeast to Spotsylvania Court House, a dozen miles closer to Richmond. On May 10 the Yankees fiercely attacked Lee's new defense line. "I intend to fight it out on this line if it takes all summer," Grant stubbornly informed Washington. The brutal attack continued on to May 12 when the Yankees finally broke through the Rebel

defenses. "The men . . . rushed on through the forest
shouting like mad men, shooting at every fleeing Confederate they saw," Union Lieutenant Colonel Charles
Weygant exclaimed.

Confederate Major General John B. Gordon hurriedly sent three Rebel brigades charging at the wave of
oncoming Yankees. General Lee recklessly rode forward
to give courage to the troops. "General Lee to the rear!"
the Rebels shouted. Soldiers grabbed the bridle of his
horse and led their beloved general away from danger. As
Gordon's men plunged into the battle, the slaughter
continued in a soaking rainstorm.

More than 20,000 Union and Confederate troops
were lost in the two days of fighting at Spotsylvania. In

Union General U.S. Grant rides among his troops on May 7, 1864
after the bloody Battle of the Wilderness. Yankee soldiers cheered
when they learned they would not be retreating northward. Instead
they shifted closer toward Richmond and fought again at
Spotsylvania Court House.

On the road to Cold Harbor, Virginia, General Grant and other
Union officers stop to rest in the yard at Massaponax Church, on
June 2, 1864. Smoking a cigar, Grant is seated in the pew in front
of the two trees. General George G. Meade wearing a hat with the
brim turned down (seated in the pew at the far left) carefully studies
a map.

the early hours of May 13, Lee at last ordered his exhausted army to fall back. Grant's Yankees now raced forty miles south to a dusty crossroads called Cold Harbor. Lee got there first and ordered his men to entrench. On the night of June 2, 1864, Union veterans sensed what was coming. "The men were calmly writing their names and addresses on slips of paper and pinning them to the backs of their coats," Union Lieutenant Colonel Horace Porter noted, "so that their bodies might be recognized and their fate made known to their families at home."[5]

At 4:30 A.M. June 3, buglers sounded the advance. More than 50,000 Yankee infantrymen charged the entrenched Confederates, several hundred yards away across the open ground. More than 5,600 Union men fell in just fifteen horrifying minutes. The fire, recalled Captain Charles Currier of the 40th Massachusetts, "piled up our men like cordwood." Grant quickly halted the costly head-on attack. In six weeks of steady combat, Grant had lost 50,000 men. Many Northerners now called him "The Butcher." But Grant kept going. Under cover of darkness, he slipped his army out of its trenches and crossed the James River. His target now was Petersburg, Virginia.

The Shenandoah in Flames

To take pressure off his battered army, Robert E. Lee sent 10,000 Rebels under Lieutenant General Jubal Early hurrying north into the Shenandoah Valley. Soon Early's men crossed the Potomac River and marched toward

Washington. On July 11, 1864, Early surveyed Fort Stevens, the northernmost of Washington's defensive works. Beyond them he could see the dome of the U.S. Capitol, five miles away, shimmering in the July heat. Fewer than 10,000 Union troops, inexperienced gunners and home guard soldiers, defended Washington. By mid-afternoon, however, the blue uniforms of 15,000 additional Yankees began filling the Federal lines. Grant had hurried a full corps of the Army of the Potomac northward to protect the capital. That night Early wisely ordered his army to withdraw into Virginia. "Major, we haven't taken Washington," he told one officer, "but we've scared Abe Lincoln like hell!"

General Grant swiftly ordered thirty-three-year-old Major General Philip Sheridan to drive Early out of the Shenandoah Valley. On September 19, 1864, Sheridan attacked Early's 10,000 Rebels with 45,000 men. "We have just sent them awhirling through Winchester, and we are after them tomorrow," Sheridan excitedly reported. On September 22, he defeated Early again at Fisher's Hill, chasing the weary Confederates even farther southward. To rob the Rebels of any future use of the Valley, Sheridan ruthlessly ordered his cavalry to torch every barn, granary, haystack, and mill they found. Soon pillars of black smoke darkened the sky. "I have destroyed over 2,000 barns filled with wheat, hay, and farming implements; [and] over 70 mills. . . . have driven in front of the army 4,000 head of stock and have killed . . . 3,000 sheep," Sheridan reported as his troops marched southward.[6]

On October 10, Sheridan's army encamped along Cedar Creek, near Middletown, Virginia. Few of them suspected that Jubal Early was looking for a chance to even the score. At 5 A.M. on October 19 Early launched a surprise attack at Cedar Creek while Sheridan himself was at Winchester, twenty miles away. The Rebels charged among the tents of the sleeping Yankees. The startled Union soldiers "jumped up running and did not take time to put on their clothing, but fled in their night clothes, without their guns, hats or shoes," recalled Georgia Private G. W. Nichols.

Alerted by the distant roar of cannon, Sheridan galloped southward. On his big black horse, Rienzi, the fiery little general neared Cedar Creek in the afternoon. The Yankees fleeing along the Valley turnpike stopped and cheered when they saw their gallant leader. Sheridan waved his cap and pointed them back to the front. "Forward boys! Follow me! We'll sleep in the old camp tonight!" he yelled. Thrilled by Sheridan's fighting spirit, the Yankees reformed their battle line and soon sent Early's men running. Sheridan's stirring victory at Cedar Creek closed the Shenandoah Valley forever to the Rebels.

We are not fighting hostile armies, but a hostile people, and must make old and young, rich and poor, feel the hard hand of war.
    —William Tecumseh Sherman, 1864

7 Collapse of the Confederacy

 "I can . . . make Georgia howl!" General William T. Sherman promised. To destroy the enemy's will to fight, in November 1864 Sherman suggested a bold sweeping move, a march from Atlanta to Savannah, "smashing things to the sea."

Sherman's March

On the evening of November 15, 1864 the Yankee invaders put Atlanta to the torch. Great sheets of roaring flame towered hundreds of feet above the rooftops. Huge clouds of swirling sparks and floating cinders choked the air. Two hundred acres of Atlanta stores, houses, railroad buildings, and machine-shops collapsed in burnt ruins.

Leaving General George Thomas behind to defend

Union General William Tecumseh Sherman (1820-1891) on horseback in Atlanta. Sherman's concept of total warfare included burning Atlanta and marching his army across Georgia, destroying everything in its path. His tough, hard marching soldiers fondly called him "Uncle Billy."

Tennessee, Sherman marched southward, his 62,000 men in two great columns. Row upon row of gun barrels glistened in the blazing Georgia sun. The Yankees traveled lightly, each foot soldier carrying a musket and bayonet and eighty rounds of ammunition. Without a base of supplies, Sherman depended on the bounty of Georgia to feed his hungry men. On the march he ordered that every brigade send a daily party of soldiers out to gather food. These men, called "bummers," swarmed over the countryside. One plantation owner, Dolly Sumner Lunt Burge, recalled with horror, "Like Demons they rushed in! My yards are full. To my smoke-house, my Dairy, Pantry, Kitchen and Cellar, like famished wolves they come. . . . The thousand pounds of meat in my smoke-house is gone in a twinkling, my flour, my meat, my lard, butter, eggs, pickles . . . are all gone."[1]

The Yankees marched through Georgia's capital of Milledgeville and continued southward. Every day African American slaves thronged the roadsides and greeted the bluecoats with roaring cheers. Then they gathered up their bundles and followed after the army. "They thought it was freedom now or never," remembered an Illinois artilleryman. Day after day Sherman's columns swept forward, meeting little resistance from the Rebel enemy. "The weather was fine, the roads good and everything seemed to favor us," Sherman later remembered.

By December 13, 1864, Sherman's soldiers could smell the salt air of the Atlantic Ocean. Charging Yankees captured Fort McAllister outside of Savannah and on December 21 marched into that defenseless city. In less than a month Sherman's men had sliced the South in two, leaving a path of destruction sixty miles wide and three hundred miles long. Behind them 317 miles of railroad track had been twisted around trees. The charred ruins of mills, factories, and farms filled the Georgia landscape. The Union army had seized 6,871 mules and horses and 13,294 head of cattle. It had captured or destroyed millions of pounds of grains and other food supplies. "We had laid a heavy hand on Georgia," remarked Union army surgeon J. C. Patton.

Having seized Savannah, in January Sherman next ordered his Union army north into the Carolinas.

Plantation slaves packed their possessions and excitedly followed after Sherman's army. General Sherman later recalled, "...the Negroes were simply frantic with joy. Whenever they heard my name, they clustered about my horse, shouted and prayed....I have witnessed hundreds, if not thousands, of such scenes."

Hell in Tennessee

While Sherman struck southward, Confederate General John Bell Hood marched north into Tennessee. At Franklin on November 30, 1864, Hood found Major General John Schofield's Union army of 34,000. "We will make the fight," Hood vowed. Thirteen times, Hood recklessly sent his Rebels across open fields toward the entrenched Union lines. In the resulting slaughter, six Confederate generals died. "It was awful!" Confederate Lieutenant Colonel William D. Gale exclaimed of the battle. "The ditch at the enemy's line . . . was literally

Yankee soldiers destroy a Georgia railroad. After tearing up the iron rails, they lay them on piles of burning wooden ties. Then they bent the hot rails around trees and called them "Sherman's neckties."

filled with dead bodies." Hood lost 6,300 men, more than one-eighth of his army.

That night Schofield quietly marched his Yankees northward to Nashville where they joined General Thomas, swelling Thomas's force to more than 50,000. Stubbornly, Hood also marched to Nashville, but with only 30,000 Rebels. On December 15, Thomas lashed out in attack, smashing Hood's left flank the next day. "My men were amongst them capturing them right and left," declared Iowa Colonel John H. Stibbs. "In less time than it takes to tell it, we had captured guns, caisson colors, and prisoners galore."

"The army was panic-stricken," exclaimed Rebel Private Sam Watkins. "The woods everywhere were full of running soldiers. Our officers were crying 'Halt! Halt!' "[2] The Battle of Nashville cost the Confederates 5,400 men. Hood's Army of Tennessee was destroyed. The Rebels who survived his reckless leadership trudged southward in defeat, singing with grim humor of how "The gallant Hood of Texas played hell in Tennessee."

In the Petersburg Trenches

"Our matters here are at a deadlock," wrote Union Major Washington Roebling in the summer of 1864. "Everyone knows that if Lee were to come out of his trenchments we could whip him, but Bob Lee is a little too smart for us." At Petersburg, Virginia, sweating Yankees and Rebels using picks and shovels threw up dirt-walled forts and dug trenches. Mule teams dragged forward rifled siege guns and heavy mortars capable of lofting shells great distances. Musketry cracked across "no man's land" whenever a soldier showed his head. The two enemies settled in for a long siege. Although Grant forced Lee's Rebels to thin their lines by continually edging farther southwestward, the Yankees could not break them.

The Yankees of the 48th Pennsylvania Regiment, most of them former coal miners, suggested one plan to break the Rebel lines. They offered to dig a five-hundred-foot tunnel beneath the Confederate lines and pack it with four tons of gunpowder. The object was to blow a hole in the Petersburg defenses, then charge through and capture the town. General Grant agreed to give the plan a try. Working in shifts around the clock, the Pennsylvania miners were soon burrowing 40 feet a day through sand and clay. When they finished on July 27, they loaded the tunnel with 320 kegs of gunpowder.

At dawn on July 30 the fuse was lit. Union Major Oliver C. Bosbyshell, witnessed the mighty explosion. "A vast cloud of earth is borne upward, one hundred feet in the air . . . descending in the twinkling of an eye with a heavy thud!" The blast tore a great crater into the ground, 30 feet deep, 70 feet wide, and 250 feet long, and killed nearly 300 Rebels. Rocks, beams, timbers, and mangled human bodies filled the surrounding landscape.

With a yell, 10,000 attacking Yankees stormed into the hole. There was no way beyond the sheer, thirty-foot walls of the crater, however. As the Union troops crowded close, the Confederates mounted a counterattack and began pouring fire down upon them. The

Rebels were enraged to discover African-American soldiers among the U.S. troops. "I saw Confederates beating and shooting at the [helpless] negro soldiers," recalled Virginia Private George S. Bernard. Some of the Yankees fought to the death; others tried to surrender, while thousands simply ran for their lives. By 2:00 P.M. the Battle of the Crater was over. The Yankees suffered 3,500 men killed, wounded, or missing, compared with Confederate losses of about 1,500. "It was the saddest affair I have witnessed in the War," Grant later admitted.

Flight to Appomattox

Over the next eight long months, Grant and Lee faced one another along 50 miles of entrenched lines stretching from Petersburg to Richmond. Four years of constant war had broken the Confederate economy. In Richmond hungry citizens were paying $45 for a pound of coffee and $25 for a pound of butter. In the Confederate trenches sickness and desertion shrank Lee's army. "I've got no shoes, General," shouted a barefoot Rebel soldier to Lee one day. "I'm hungry, sir," another called. "We've got nothing to eat."[3]

In spite of these hardships General Lee held his position until April 1, 1865. On that day Union cavalry captured the last rail line leading into Petersburg. Before the enemy could surround his army, Lee ordered the trenches abandoned. While attending services at Richmond's St. Paul's Episcopal Church on Sunday, April 2, Confederate President Jefferson Davis received a note

Yankee soldiers in the trenches in front of Petersburg. General Grant
kept his troops well supplied and ready for action.

from Lee. "My lines are broken in three places. Richmond must be evacuated this evening."

That night Richmond citizens sadly watched the Confederate soldiers march away. Southern army surgeon James D. McCabe remembered, "At midnight the army commenced to withdraw from the trenches, and move rapidly . . . through the streets, towards the river." Rebel soldiers exploded arsenals and torched warehouses until the flames blazed out of control. By dawn the last of the Southern troops had fled westward across the James River. At the same time from the east, Union soldiers invaded the burning capital. "Company after company, regiment after regiment," observed Richmond nurse Phoebe Yates Pember, "they poured into the doomed city, an endless stream."[4] Squads of Northern troops doused the fires and patrolled the streets, bringing order to the ruined city. Most of the Yankees, however, chased the escaping Confederates.

"On and on, hour after hour," wrote Rebel general John B. Gordon, "from hilltop to hilltop, the lines were alternately forming, fighting, and retreating, making one almost continuous battle." After six days and ninety miles of marching without rest, the ragged Rebel army reached the little village of Appomattox Court House. Nearly surrounded and hopelessly outnumbered, by the morning of April 9, 1865, General Lee fully realized his situation. "There is nothing left [for] me to do but to go and see General Grant, and I would rather die a thousand deaths," he told an aide. He sent a message through the lines, requesting an interview with the Union commander.

One of Lee's staff officers, Colonel Charles Marshall, rode ahead to find a suitable meeting place. On the village street he met Wilmer McLean. Four years earlier McLean had owned a farm near Manassas, Virginia. Soldiers had trampled his crops and a cannonball had crashed through his kitchen during the First Battle of Bull Run. In search of peace, McLean had moved west to Appomattox Court House. Now McLean reluctantly offered the use of his house for the surrender meeting. Having witnessed the beginning of the war, McLean now would witness its end as well. In a front parlor,

Richmond buildings stand in burnt ruins in April 1865. Rather than leave supplies behind, retreating Confederate soldiers set arsenals and warehouses on fire. Richmond resident Sallie Brock recalled the early morning hours of April 3: "From the lower portion of the city, near the river, dense black clouds of smoke arose as...devouring flames...leaped from building to building....All the railroad bridges...were in flames."

General Lee, dressed in a crisp gray uniform, waited for Grant's arrival.

Before long Grant, his boots spattered with mud, rode into the Mclean yard on his warhorse Cincinnati. Inside the house he greeted General Lee. The surrender terms Grant offered were simple and generous. Confederate officers could keep their side arms and personal possessions; officers and men who claimed to own their horses could keep them, too; and "each officer and man will be allowed to return to his home, not to be disturbed by the United States authorities."[5]

Just before four o'clock, General Grant and General Lee signed the necessary papers. Lee shook hands with Grant and bowed to the other Union officers in the room and left. Mounting his horse Traveller, Lee slowly rode off to the Confederate camp just north of the town. Riding toward his own lines, General Grant soon heard Union cannon firing salutes at the glorious news of surrender. Immediately he ordered that this loud celebration be stopped. "The war is over," he stated, "the rebels are our countrymen again." He saw no reason to shame the brave Southerners at the moment of their surrender.

That evening outside his headquarters tent, Lee briefly spoke to his gathered troops. "Boys, I have done the best I could for you. Go home now, and if you make as good citizens as you have soldiers, you will do well, and I shall always be proud of you." On April 12, 1865, Lee's 28,231 remaining Confederate troops marched into Appomattox Court House between two long rows of Union troops. At "Surrender Triangle," where three

The Wilmer McLean house at Appomattox Court House, Virginia. In McLean's front parlor Robert E. Lee surrendered his Confederate army to U.S. Grant on April 9, 1865. Afterwards Union officers stole McLean's parlor furniture for souvenirs. Brigadier General George A. Custer rode off with a small table.

roads crossed, the men piled their muskets and furled their battle flags in a formal surrender ceremony. Many Confederate soldiers wept. Afterwards they started for their homes. For them the war was over.

Assassination

As word spread of Lee's surrender, people cheered in the streets of Washington, D.C., and strangers hugged one another. In a speech he gave from a White House balcony, Lincoln spoke of his desire to reunite the country quickly.

The people of Washington greeted the morning of April 14, 1865, Good Friday, with feelings of peace and hope. At least one man, however, plotted the murder of Abraham Lincoln. Twenty-six-year-old John Wilkes Booth was a popular stage actor from a family of famous actors. Born in the border state of Maryland, Booth identified with the South. Secretly he wished to make himself famous by doing something to help the Confederacy. Drawing an odd group of conspirators about him in 1864, Booth first plotted to kidnap President Lincoln but failed twice to carry out his plans. As the war rushed to its end in April of 1865, Booth madly vowed to kill Lincoln at the very first opportunity.

His chance arrived on April 14 when he learned that Lincoln would be attending a play at Ford's Theater that night. That evening 1,700 people filled Ford's Theater expecting a carefree time. The play was a comedy, *Our American Cousin,* starring Laura Keene. Lincoln and his wife Mary sat in a private box at the right-hand side of the stage along with their guests Major Henry Rathbone and his fiancée Miss Clara Harris.

Shortly after ten o'clock John Wilkes Booth slipped into the narrow passage that led to the president's box. Groping forward in the darkness, Booth timed his movements carefully. During a particularly loud moment on stage, he opened the box door, stepped behind the president, and pulled the trigger of a derringer pistol. The bullet struck Lincoln behind the left ear and smashed deep within his skull.

Gunsmoke clouded the air as Major Rathbone jumped up and grappled with the murderer. Booth slashed Rathbone's arm with a hunting knife. Then he climbed over the box railing and leaped down to the stage. Booth's right boot caught on a flag hanging from the box, causing him to land awkwardly and break his left leg above the ankle. Shouting *"Sic Semper Tyrannis!"* (meaning "Thus always with tyrants!", the motto of the state of Virginia), the crazed actor limped hurriedly away. In the alley behind the theater, Booth leaped onto his waiting horse and galloped off into the night.

Soldiers slowly carried the limp and bloodied president across the street to William Petersen's boardinghouse. In a small room at the far end of the hall they gently laid him on a bed. That night cabinet members, congressmen, and friends of Lincoln crowded into the little room. They knew their beloved leader could not survive. At 7:22 A.M., April 15, 1865, Abraham Lincoln breathed his last. John Hay, the president's personal secretary, observed that "a look of unspeakable peace came over his worn features."[6] The men in the room stood with bowed heads when Lincoln died, and Secretary of War Edwin Stanton sadly uttered, "Now he belongs to the ages."

Clicking telegraph keys swiftly spread the news of Lincoln's assassination. Newspapers edged with black headlined the shocking story. Church bells tolled in city and town. With deep bitterness Northerners blamed the entire South for the bloody murder and demanded harsh revenge. At the moment of the North's greatest triumph, cruel feelings again settled over the land.

*With malice toward none; with charity for
all . . . let us strive on to finish the work we
are in; to bind up the nation's wounds.*
    —from Abraham Lincoln's second inaugural address,
    March 4, 1865

8 The Aftermath

 Union cavalrymen galloped in all directions.
The United States government had offered
great rewards for the capture of John Wilkes Booth. Cornered at last on April 25 in a tobacco barn near Bowling
Green, Virginia, Booth refused to surrender. Soldiers set
fire to the barn. As Booth hopped around inside on
crutches, Sergeant Boston Corbett spied him through a
crack and shot him in the neck. Within a few hours Lincoln's killer was dead.

In May, 1865, Washington citizens jammed a courtroom to watch the military trial of eight other suspects in
Booth's kidnapping and murder plots. Four of them—
Samuel Arnold, Michael O'Laughlin, Edward Spangler
(a Ford's Theater stagehand), and Samuel Mudd (the

The hanging of the Lincoln conspirators (left to right) Mary Surratt, Lewis Paine, David Herold, and George Atzerodt. These executions occurred at Washington's Arsenal Penitentiary on July 7, 1865. To shade themselves from the sun, some spectators carried umbrellas.

Maryland doctor who set Booth's broken leg)—received prison terms. The court condemned the other four— David Herold, George Atzerodt, Lewis Paine (who slashed Secretary of State William Seward with a knife on the night of Lincoln's murder), and Mary Surratt (who owned the boardinghouse where Booth and his plotters often met)—to death. On July 7, hangmen fixed nooses around their necks, released the spring trapdoors, and watched them drop to their deaths.

The war was finally over by this time. The last Confederate generals had followed Lee's example and surrendered their armies. Joseph Johnston surrendered to Sherman at the Bennett farmhouse near Durham, North Carolina, on April 26. Rebel General Richard Taylor surrendered his army on May 4 at Citronelle, Alabama. Three weeks later the men of General E. Kirby-Smith's army laid down their arms at New Orleans.

In the early dawn of May 10, 1865, Yankee cavalrymen on patrol galloped into the woods near Irwinsville, Georgia. In a small camp of tents and wagons they came upon and captured Confederate President Jefferson Davis. During the war Union soldiers sang of their promise to "hang Jeff Davis on a sour apple tree." Instead the Yankees sent the proud Confederate leader north where he would spend two hard years in prison.

On May 23, President Andrew Johnson and General U. S. Grant stood side by side on a reviewing stand on Washington's Pennsylvania Avenue. Thousands of excited citizens also lined the wide street. For two full days they watched the passing of a final "Grand Review" of

Grand Review of the Union armies, May 23-24, 1865. The dome of the Capital rises in the background as victorious Yankee troops march down Washington's Pennsylvania Avenue toward the White House. And when the parade was over, the soldiers returned to their homes.

150,000 Union troops. Officers saluted as they trotted by on horseback. Bayonets glistened in the sunlight as enlisted men marched past. General Meade led the men of the Army of the Potomac. General Sherman rode at the head of the Yankees who had marched through Georgia. Bands blared "The Star Spangled Banner" as the lean, sunburned soldiers passed by one last time before returning home.

The defeated Confederate soldiers returned home to find their farms in ruins and their factories burned. Out of the rubble of war the Southern states struggled to rebuild their governments during this period of "Reconstruction." On December 18, 1865, the Thirteenth Amendment to the Constitution became law. It stated that "Neither slavery nor involuntary servitude . . . shall exist within the United States." Slavery was dead forever. That year Congress also established the Freedmen's Bureau. It provided Southern African Americans with educational help, medical services, farmland, and jobs.

Many Northern politicians demanded harsh treatment for the conquered South. "The Republican party and it alone can save the Union," sourly declared Pennsylvania congressman Thaddeus Stevens. For the next eleven years Congress kept the South divided into five military districts commanded by U.S. army generals. Yankee politicians carrying luggage fashioned from carpet material swarmed into the South to run the local governments. These "carpetbaggers" were often corrupt, openly buying the support of African-American voters and robbing state treasuries.

Angry white Southerners searched for ways to regain control of their states. A secret organization called the Ku Klux Klan soon rose up throughout the South. Disguised in ghostly robes and high peaked hoods, Klansmen nightly galloped across the countryside. Burning houses and brutally attacking their enemies, they struck terror into the hearts of African Americans and carpetbaggers alike. The national peace envisioned by Abraham Lincoln had turned into a Southern nightmare. It would be many years before African Americans obtained their full civil rights.

President Andrew Johnson granted pardons to thousands of Confederates willing to take an oath of allegiance. On February 24, 1868, enraged Republicans in the House of Representatives voted to impeach Johnson for "high crimes and misdemeanors." During the spring of 1868 spectators packed the Senate gallery to witness President Johnson's Senate trial. The day of judgment arrived on May 16, 1868. The decision of the Senate was so closely split, that Johnson was found innocent by just one vote. As he finished his presidency Andrew Johnson continued to fight to carry out Abraham Lincoln's policy of fairness for the defeated South.

After his surrender, Robert E. Lee became president of Washington College (later to become Washington and Lee University) in Lexington, Virginia. Beloved throughout the South, Lee died of heart failure in 1870. During the war the U.S. government had confiscated Lee's estate in Arlington, Virginia, and thousands of Union soldiers were buried on part of that

Robert E. Lee posed for this photograph in Richmond on April 17, 1865. After the war Lee wrote, "I think it is the duty of every citizen, in the present condition of the country, to do all in his power to aid in the restoration of peace and harmony."

property. We know it today as Arlington National Cemetery.

Americans elected the military hero Ulysses S. Grant to two terms as U. S. president, beginning in 1868. Grant proved a better general than president. Though Grant himself was honest and had great personal integrity, many members of his administration took bribes and broke laws. After Grant left the White House, a business partner cheated him of his life savings. To provide for his family, Grant wrote his memoirs. He finished the best-selling book just days before he died of throat cancer in 1885 at Mount McGregor, New York.

In death, Grant and Lee joined the fallen comrades they had led in battle. One of every five soldiers and sailors in service during the war had died: more than 600,000 men altogether. Property with a value of $15 billion had been destroyed. Speaking for his generation, Supreme Court Justice and Union veteran Oliver Wendell Holmes, Jr., declared, "Our hearts were touched by fire."[1] It would take many years to heal the wounds of the Civil War. But the strength and glory of the United States today proves the cost was not too high. The years after the Civil War fulfilled the vow made by Abraham Lincoln on the battlefield of Gettysburg. In view of row upon row of the buried slain, Lincoln had solemnly promised, "We here highly resolve that these dead shall not have died in vain—that this nation, under God, shall have a new birth of freedom."

Chronology

November 6, 1860—Abraham Lincoln elected sixteenth U.S. president.

December 20, 1860—South Carolina secedes; within months ten other Southern states also left the Union.

February 9, 1861—Jefferson Davis elected president of the Confederate States of America.

April 12–13, 1861—Confederate bombardment of Fort Sumter, Charleston, South Carolina.

May 20, 1861—Richmond, Virginia, named new Confederate capital.

July 21, 1861—First Battle of Bull Run, Manassas, Virginia.

April 6–7, 1862—Battle of Shiloh, Pittsburg Landing, Tennessee.

June 25–July 1, 1862—Seven Days Battles in Virginia.

August 29–30, 1862—Second Battle of Bull Run.

September 17, 1862—Battle of Antietam, Sharpsburg, Maryland.

September 22, 1862—Lincoln issues Emancipation Proclamation.

December 13, 1862—Battle of Fredericksburg, Virginia.

December 31, 1862–January 2, 1863—Battle of Stone's River, Murfreesboro, Tennessee.

May 1–4, 1863—Battle of Chancellorsville, Virginia.

July 1–3, 1863—Battle of Gettysburg, Pennsylvania.

July 4, 1863—Confederate surrender of Vicksburg, Mississippi.

September 19–20, 1863—Battle of Chickamauga, Georgia.

November 24–25, 1863—Battle of Chattanooga, Tennessee.

May and June 1864—Grant and Lee battle in Virginia at the Wilderness, Spotsylvania Court House, and Cold Harbor.

July 1864–April 1865—Union siege of Petersburg and Richmond, Virginia.

September 2, 1864—William Tecumseh Sherman captures Atlanta, Georgia.

November 16–December 21, 1864—Sherman's march across Georgia.

April 9, 1865—Robert E. Lee surrenders to Ulysses S. Grant at Appomattox Court House, Virginia.

April 14, 1865—Abraham Lincoln assassinated at Ford's Theater.

May 23–24, 1865—Final "Grand Review" of the victorious Union armies, Washington, D.C.

Notes by Chapter

Chapter 1

1. W. A. Swanburg, *First Blood* (New York, Charles Scribner's Sons, 1957), p. 296.

2. Richard Wheeler, *Voices of the Civil War* (New York, Meridian, 1990), p. 9.

3. Mary Boykin Chestnut, *A Diary From Dixie* (Gloucester, Massachusetts, Peter Smith, 1961), p. 37.

4. Wheeler, p. 14.

Chapter 2

1. Geoffrey C. Ward, *The Civil War* (New York, Alfred A. Knopf, Inc., 1990), p. 16.

2. Truman Nelson, *The Old Man* (New York, Holt, Rinehart and Winston, 1973), p. 278.

3. Abraham Lincoln, *Speeches and Writings 1859–1865* (New York, The Library of America, 1989), pp. 223–224.

4. Richard Wheeler, *Voices of the Civil War* (New York, Meridian, 1990), p. 18.

5. Ibid., p. 28.

6. W. W. Blackford, *War Years with Jeb Stuart* (New York, Charles Scribner's Sons, 1946), p. 34.

Chapter 3

1. Bruce Catton, *Grant Moves South* (Boston, Little, Brown and Company, 1960), p. 175.

2. Sam R. Watkins, *"Co. Aytch"* (Wilmington, Delaware, Broadfoot Publishing Company, 1990), p. 66.

3. James Street, Jr., *The Struggle for Tennessee* (Alexandria, Virginia, Time-Life Books, Inc., 1985), p. 92.

4. Ulysses S. Grant, *Personal Memoirs* (New York, Charles L. Webster & Company, 1894), p. 270.

5. Samuel Carter III, *The Final Fortress* (New York, St. Martin's Press, 1980), p. 183.

6. Geoffrey C. Ward, *The Civil War* (New York, Alfred A. Knopf, Inc., 1990), p. 238.

Chapter 4

1. William C. Davis, *Duel Between the First Ironclads* (Garden City, New York, Doubleday & Company, Inc., 1975), p. 130.

2. Elisha Hunt Rhodes, *All for the Union* (New York, First Vintage Civil War Library, 1985), p. 59.

3. James V. Murfin, *The Gleam of Bayonets* (New York, A. S. Barnes and Company, Inc., 1965), p. 133.

4. Abraham Lincoln, *Speeches and Writings 1859–1865* (New York, The Library of America, 1989), p. 424.

5. William K. Goolrick, *Rebels Resurgent* (Alexandria, Virginia, Time-Life Books, Inc., 1985), pp. 76–77.

6. Richard Wheeler, *Voices of the Civil War* (New York, Meridian, 1990), p. 259.

Chapter 5

1. Geoffrey C. Ward, *The Civil War* (New York, Alfred A. Knopf, Inc., 1990), p. 244.

2. Jerry Korn, *War on the Mississippi* (Alexandria, Virginia, Time-Life Books, Inc., 1985), p. 95.

3. W. W. Blackford, *War Years with Jeb Stuart* (New York, Charles Scribner's Sons, 1946), pp. 27–28.

4. Phoebe Yates Pember, *A Southern Woman's Story* (St. Simons Island, Georgia, Mockingbird Books, Inc., 1990), p. 115.

5. Neal Dow, "A General Behind Bars: Neal Dow in Libby Prison" (edited by Frank L. Byrne). In William B. Hesseltine (Ed.), *Civil War Prisons* (Kent, Ohio, The Kent State University Press, 1962), p. 65.

6. Abraham Lincoln, *Speeches and Writings 1859–1865* (New York, The Library of America, 1989), p. 536.

Chapter 6

1. Jerry Korn, *The Fight for Chattanooga* (Alexandria, Virginia, Time-Life Books, Inc., 1985), p. 61.

2. Harry Hansen, *The Civil War* (New York, New American Library, 1961), p. 475.

3. Ronald H. Bailey, *Battles for Atlanta* (Alexandria, Virginia, Time-Life Books, Inc., 1985), p. 60.

4. Richard Wheeler, *Voices of the Civil War* (New York, Meridian, 1990), pp. 383–384.

5. Noah Andre Trudeau, *Bloody Roads South* (Boston, Little, Brown and Company, 1989), p. 280.

6. Geoffrey C. Ward, *The Civil War* (New York, Alfred A. Knopf, Inc., 1990), p. 333.

Chapter 7

1. David Nevin, *Sherman's March* (Alexandria, Virginia, Time-Life Books, Inc., 1986), p. 54.

2. Sam R. Watkins, *"Co. Aytch"* (Wilmington, Delaware, Broadfoot Publishing Company, 1990), p. 224.

3. Burke Davis, *To Appomattox* (New York, Rinehart & Company, Inc., 1959), p. 20.

4. Phoebe Yates Pember, *A Southern Woman's Story* (St. Simons Island, Georgia, Mockingbird Books, Inc., 1990), p. 95.

5. Davis, p. 384.

6. John G. Nicolay and John Hay, *Abraham Lincoln, Volume Ten* (New York, The Century Co., 1890), pp. 301–302.

Chapter 8

1. Geoffrey C. Ward, *The Civil War* (New York, Alfred A. Knopf, Inc., 1990), p. 394.

Further Reading

Catton, Bruce. *The Battle of Gettysburg.* New York: American Heritage Publishing Co., 1963.

Davis, Burke. *Appomattox Closing Struggle of the Civil War.* New York: Harper & Row Publishers, 1963.

Freedman, Russell. *Lincoln a Photography.* New York: Clarion Books, 1987.

Grant, Ulysses S. *Personal Memoirs.* New York: Charles L. Webster & Company, 1894.

Kent, Zachary. *Ulysses S. Grant.* Chicago, Children's Press, Inc., 1989.

Meltzer, Milton. *Voices from the Civil War.* New York: Thomas Y. Crowell, 1989.

Murphy, Jim. *The Boy's War.* New York: Clarion Books, 1990.

Ray, Delia. *A Nation Torn.* New York: Lodestar Books, 1990.

Shaara, Michael. *The Killer Angels.* New York: Ballantine Books, 1974.

Internet Sites

The American Civil War
http://americancivilwar.com/

The American Civil War Homepage
http://sunsite.utk.edu/civil-war/warweb.html

The Civil War Homepage
http://www.civil-war.net/

Civil War Maps—Library of Congress
http://memory.loc.gov/ammem/gmdhtml/cwmhtml/cwmhome.html

Civil War Photographs—Library of Congress
http://memory.loc.gov/ammem/cwphtml/cwphome.html

The History Place—A Nation Divided:
U. S. Civil War 1861–1865
http://www.historyplace.com/civilwar/index.html

Shotgun's Home of the American Civil War
http://www.civilwarhome.com/index.htm

United States Civil War
http://www.us-civilwar.com/

WWW.CivilWar.Com
http://www.civilwar.com

Index